P9-DNV-685

The Elementary Principles of CHRIST

The Elementary Principles of CHRIST

PAUL C. JONG

Hephzibah Publishing House
A Ministry of THE NEW LIFE MISSION
SEOUL, KOREA

The Elementary Principles of CHRIST

Scripture quotations are from *the New King James Version.*

ISBN 89-8314-369-X
Cover Art by Min-soo Kim
Illustration by Young-ae Kim
Printed in Korea

Hephzibah Publishing House
A Ministry of THE NEW LIFE MISSION
48 Bon-dong, Dongjack-gu
Seoul, Korea 156-060

♠ Website: http://www.nlmission.com
http://www.bjnewlife.org
♠ E-mail: newlife@bjnewlife.org
♠ Phone: 82(Korea)-11-1788-2954
♠ Fax: 82-33-637-4440

The Analysis of The Apostles' Creed

Confession of Faith in God, the Father

"I believe in God the Father Almighty, Maker of heaven and earth,"

Confession of Faith in God the Son

"I believe in Jesus Christ, His only Son our Lord,
who was conceived by the Holy Ghost,
born of the Virgin Mary,
suffered under Pontius Pilate, was crucified,
died, and was buried;
He descended into hell;
The third day He rose again from the dead;
He ascended into heaven, and sitteth on the right hand of God the Father Almighty; from thence
He shall come to judge the quick and the dead."

Confession of Faith in the Holy Spirit

"I believe in the Holy Ghost,
the holy catholic Church, the communion of saints;
the forgiveness of sins;
the resurrection of the body;
and the life everlasting. Amen."

Table of Contents

PART 3

The Law

Preface

As I spread the gospel of the water and the Spirit all over the world along with my colleagues, I have come to realize the fact that it is urgent to help souls to correctly establish the foundations of the faith first. In particular, when we tried to reach the unreached with the gospel of the water and the Spirit, who had served other gods, I often found that the gospel could not take root in their hearts due to the lack of true knowledge of God. This is the first reason why I started to write this book.

The Apostles' Creed is a summary of the Apostles' faith. The Apostles believed that the Triune God (the Father, the Son, and the Holy Spirit) created all creatures. They believed that Jesus Christ, God the Son, saved all of mankind from their sins by coming to this world in flesh, by His baptism and His crucifixion. They believe that He gives resurrection and eternal life in the Kingdom of Heaven to those with faith.

The essence of such faith can be affirmed by the early church and the Apostles once again in Hebrews 6:1-2. In other words, we can affirm that the Apostles believed and preached the Word of God concerning repentance from dead works, faith toward God, the doctrine of baptism and laying on of hands, resurrection of the dead, and eternal judgment as the elementary principles of Christ. What we need to observe here is that the Apostles spread the principles of the gospel as they associated 'the laying on of hands' of the sacrificial system with 'the baptism that Jesus received.'

Also, right before the Lord ascended, He commanded the disciples "*Go therefore and make disciples of all the nations, baptizing them in the name of the Father and of the Son and of the Holy Spirit" (Matthew 28:19).* This is to make disciples of those who believe in Jesus' baptism and baptize them in the name of God in three Persons.

Therefore, the faith of the Apostles was established within the "gospel of the water and the Spirit". Unfortunately, today's faith of Christianity is very different from the faith of the Apostles. In truth, we cannot find the faith in 'Jesus' baptism' that is so important in today's faith of Christianity. What is worse, among theologians and preachers, there are many who deny even the divinity of Jesus. This is the second reason why I started to write this book.

The Apostles' faith is a valuable lesson to those of us who believe in God. We now must understand the righteousness of God and return to the true faith. We all are those who can possess the righteous faith in the gospel of the water and the Spirit that the Apostles possessed. ⊠

Paul C. Jong

PART I

I. CONFESSION OF FAITH IN GOD THE FATHER

"I believe in God the Father Almighty, Maker of heaven and earth,"

God the Father

There are three confessions manifested in the Apostles' faith.

The first confession is that they believed in God the Father Almighty, the Creator of the heavens and the earth (Genesis 1:1); secondly, they confessed that Jesus Christ the Son of God had given them the remission of their sins; and the third confession is that they believed that Jesus Christ was conceived of the Holy Spirit. We must also confess that we believe in God the Father, the Son, and the Holy Spirit, for we must have the same faith as the Apostles.

For us, the Father is God, just as the Son and the Holy Spirit are also God. Insofar as the essence of the Father, the Son, and the Holy Spirit is concerned, they are all the same God, as our faith in them is the same faith. For instance, because the Father is the Almighty God, the Son is also the Almighty God. The three Persons of the Holy Trinity, in other words, are in their essence the same God. We thus believe accordingly, that the three Persons of the Father, the Son, and the Holy Spirit are fundamentally and completely one. As such, in order for us to build the foundation of our faith in the Word of God, we must be anchored in this Word of truth.

Scriptural Evidence

1. From the Old Testament

(1) First of all, the Old Testament clearly shows that God is one: *"Hear, O Israel: The LORD our God, the LORD is one!" (Deuteronomy 6:4).*

(2) At the same time, however, the Old Testament also tells us unmistakably that God exists in several persons: *"Then God said, 'Let Us make man in Our image, according to Our likeness..." (Genesis 1:26); "'Come, let Us go down there and confuse their language, that they may not understand one another's speech'" (Genesis 11:7).* From these passages we can see and believe that God exists not in single person but in multiple persons.

2. From the New Testament

The Father, the Son, and the Holy Spirit are God to us. But God exists in three independent persons. This truth is revealed in unequivocal terms also in the New Testament.

(1) That the Father, the Son, and the Holy Spirit exist as separate persons is clearly evidenced by the account of Jesus' baptism that marked the beginning of His ministry: *"When He had been baptized, Jesus came up immediately from the water; and behold, the heavens were opened to Him, and He saw the Spirit of God descending like a dove and lighting upon Him. And suddenly a voice came from heaven, saying, 'This is My*

beloved Son, in whom I am well pleased'" (Matthew 3:16-7).

This passage describes the baptism of Jesus by John the Baptist, when the Triune God is revealed. From this passage we know that Jesus is the Son of God, that the Holy Spirit works with Him, and that the Father declared Him to be "His beloved Son, in whom He is well pleased." Through these manifestations the Triune God is revealed. Jesus could fulfill all the righteousness of God because He took all the sins of mankind with His baptism received from John. This is why He had to die on the Cross for us, and this is "the righteousness of God" that the Father fulfilled through His Son. That Jesus took all our sins on Him by His righteous act of baptism is the very righteousness of God, and this truth is affirmed by both the Father and the Holy Spirit. Thus, the Father, the Son, and the Holy Spirit exist as separate persons, but are the same God for us.

(2) Matthew 28:19 also reveals that the Father, the Son, and the Holy Spirit are one God, as Jesus commanded His disciples to *"make disciples of all the nations, baptizing them in the name of the Father and of the Son and of the Holy Spirit"*—that is, in names of the three separate persons of the Trinity.

The Father, the Son, and the Holy Spirit are each an independent person, but at the same time they are the same in that they all are the same God. As such, when we believe in God, we believe in one God as the united entity of the three persons.

God the Father, the Son, and the Holy Spirit as professed by the Christian faith is the self-existing God, different from all other deities. Some other religions believe that Jesus is only one of the many prophets, but this is simply not true.

For us, God is the Father, the Son, and the Holy Spirit.

Despite the fact that this truth is readily and sufficiently attested by the Scriptures, there are many who do not realize this. This is so because those who do not know the gospel of the water and the Spirit approach the concept of Holy Trinity with their human rationality and logic, which makes them impossible to understand. Those who are not born again cannot understand the Triune God. But for those of us who are born again, God the Father, the Son, and the Holy Spirit is our one God, in whom we place our absolute faith.

God's Name

"And God said to Moses, 'I AM WHO I AM.' And He said, 'Thus you shall say to the children of Israel, 'I AM has sent me to you'" (Exodus 3:14).

"Yahweh." Appearing in the Scriptures for over 5,300 times, Yahweh is the most common name by which God revealed Himself to mankind. The Jewish people held God's name as sacred, and they were very careful in invoking or calling Him by His name (Exodus 3:14). Bestowing great respect upon the name of Yahweh, they later adopted and used another name, Adonai, to call upon God. The meaning of this name is the Lord of all, in the following manner: 1) One that exists; 2) One that is the Lord of life; and 3) One that always was, always is, and will be exist forever by Himself.

We call God as the Father, the Son, and the Holy Spirit. The name of the Son of God the Father is Jesus Christ. This name means He who saves His people from their sins.

The Apostles' Creed and Its Blessings of Faith

Our desire is that the Apostles' faith be handed down to us in its unadulterated purity. This is our wish, and the hope of every Christian. Their faith should have been handed down to us sufficiently in written texts after their death. However, the true faith of the Apostles is revealed only in their Epistles, and this is why we are struggling to share and spread their faith.

What, then, is the faith of the Apostles? Strictly speaking, the Apostles' Creed was made after the passing of the Apostolic Age. It is, in other words, a testament of the Apostles' faith recorded by the generation who came after them.

The Apostles' faith is the faith in the works of the Father, the Son, and the Holy Spirit. The baptism that we receive when we accept God as our Savior requires from us the faith that confesses the following: that Jesus' baptism has cleansed all our sins; that through the blood of Jesus Christ on the Cross all our sins were accordingly judged; and that Jesus was sent by His Father as the Savior of sinners. Thus, when one believes that all his/her sins are redeemed by the baptism and blood of Jesus, he/she then receives the Holy Spirit from God.

We can therefore ask the following question to those who wish to be baptized: "Do you believe that when Jesus was baptized by John, all your sins were taken from you and placed on His shoulder instead?" When the answer is, "Yes, I believe that all my sins and all the sins of the world were taken upon by Jesus," we follow with another question: "Do you then believe that Jesus, having shouldered all your sins by being baptized by John, shed His blood on the Cross?" Those who answer affirmatively are then baptized in the name of the Father, and of the Son, and of the Holy Spirit.

Faith in the Triune God begins with the confession, "I believe in God, the Father Almighty, the Creator of heaven and earth." Only to those who believe and confess this, the Apostles could baptize them in the name of the Father, the Son, and the Holy Spirit. The true Christian faith was granted to only those who believed in the gospel of the water and the Spirit. That is why God's Church was built upon the foundation of the twelve disciples' faith.

The origins of the Apostles' Creed go back to the Edict of Milan in 313 A.D., signed by the Roman Emperor Constantine. Given the historical background to the changed status of Christianity, turning from an outlawed religion to the official, state religion of the Roman Empire, this radical change generated significant and growing interests in Christianity among all Romans. What was needed then was a standard of faith for these new believers wishing to become a part of God's Church.

The Apostles' Creed has its origins in this need, and owes its existence to the people who came after the Apostolic Age. Its present form was handed down to us after being compiled and repeatedly revised by various religious councils that followed the Apostolic Age. This is why the present Apostles' Creed must be reinterpreted through the faith in the gospel of the water and the Spirit, the differentiated faith of Christianity and the true faith. To spread this Christian faith throughout the world, we must know and believe how Jesus took the sins of mankind upon Himself, how He made these sins disappear, and how He has given human beings their eternal life.

But there are countless religions in the world. And each religion has its own deities. The difference between these deities and the Christian God is that while the former are merely human constructions, the latter is the God who exists by Himself. To believe in the Christian God, one must abandon all these false gods of the man-made religions. Without this, all efforts are fruitless. The reason why we see before our eyes such a confusion of faith about God is because of the lack of knowledge in the Creator God and His name.

In the Mongolian Empire there was a god called "Buruhung." This god is not said to have created the world, yet the Mongolians still worship "Buruhung" as their god even to this day. As such, even as they believe in the Christian God as their own God, they also believe in their national god. This makes them impossible to have true faith. If one believes that the Christian God is the same as their national god, he cannot meet the true God professed by the Christian faith. This is why we must bear witness to the Triune God of Christianity.

Why is it so hard for the true Christian faith in God to enter into all the nations of the world? It is because many of them cannot distinguish the difference between their gods and the Christian God; the Father, the Son, and the Holy Spirit. This other reason of such difficulty is that Christianity has failed to keep and preach the truth of the remission of sin, the gospel of the water and the Spirit throughout its history.

Christianity that was introduced into the Mongolian Empire made too many compromises with the existing national religion, so as to avoid any conflict of faith with the dominant Buddhist doctrines, and this resulted in the failure of the Christian truth to blossom. The Christian truth of atonement cannot be made compatible with the Buddhist doctrines. This truth of atonement means that Jesus took upon all the sins of the world for the sake of mankind, died on the Cross in our stead, rose from the dead again, and has thereby saved those who believe in Him.

But one of the Buddhist doctrines is an aversion to killing. The core truth of Christianity is the gospel of the water and the Spirit, and this truth entails Jesus' baptism of the bearing of sin and His bloodshed on the Cross. But because of the Buddhist doctrine that prohibits any killing, the Word of the bearing of sin and the death of Jesus could not be accepted or believed as it was. The Christian doctrine of atonement, therefore, could not coexist with the Buddhist doctrine of conscience.

As a result, Christianity in the Mongolian Empire eventually ended up becoming absorbed by Buddhism, and it can no longer be found in Mongolia. When the Church in the Mongolian Empire faced tribulations and persecutions, moreover, many Christians fled to Buddhist temples with little hesitation and easily converted themselves to Buddhism, and thus leading to the eventual demise of Christianity in that nation.

The biggest reason as to why Christianity disappeared from the Mongolian Empire has to do with the fact that the Mongolian faith in the Triune God was not certain. They saw "Buddha" and Jesus as the same God. This is what led to the eventual disappearance of Christianity from the Mongolian Empire.

Eternal life can come about only to those who are saved from their sins by believing in the true God of Christianity as their own God, regardless of who and where they are. We must therefore believe in the gospel of the water and the Spirit, and in the Triune God. These are the foundation of our faith in God's Church, and we must also bear witness to this truth. This truth is none other than the faith of the Apostles that this book speaks of. There is only one God in the entire world, and He is the Triune God. His name is "Yahweh," or "Jesus the Savior," or the Holy Spirit. He is the true God not only for Christians, but also for all the religious.

Who Are the Apostles?

Since the Creed is called the Apostles' Creed, we need to first find out who these Apostles were. The word Apostle means one who is sent forth. In Greek the word is *"apostolos,"* meaning a representative delegate who is entrusted with a mission. Strictly speaking, however, the title of Apostle is reserved only for the twelve disciples called upon by Jesus. But in a broader sense, it was applied to other eminent Christian teachers such as Barnabas (Acts 14:14).

Qualifications and Duties of the Apostles

(1) Those who directly received the calling by Christ to spread the gospel of the water and the Spirit (Mark 3:13; Luke 6:13; Galatians 1:1).

(2) Those who lived with Christ and witnessed His works on earth. The disciples of Jesus Christ were witnesses to the fulfillment of the righteousness of God through Christ's life

(Acts 1:21-22; 1 Corinthians 9:1).

(3) Those who, being filled by the Holy Spirit, received the power to fulfill the works commanded by Christ (Acts 15:28; 1 Corinthians 2:13; 1 Thessalonians 4:8; 1 John 5:9-12).

(4) Those who were given the power to perform miracles to bear witness to the gospel of the water and the Spirit on this earth. God gave great power to the Apostles so that Jesus Christ may be revealed through them as God the Savior (Acts 9:40; 2 Corinthians 12:12; Hebrews 2:4).

(5) Those who received a special calling, as well as special blessings, from God (Acts 9:15; 2 Corinthians 1:1; Galatians 2:8).

The authority given to the Apostles is the authority to forgive people's sins, and as such, ignoring those who have this authority will lead to one's destruction.

Do Jews Believe in God as the Father of Creation?

Jews believe in God, the Creator of the universe, who rules over the life and death of mankind and the rise and fall of nations, as their Father. In the Old Testament, God's name is called "Elohim" or "Jehovah," but in the New Testament it is Jesus Christ who is called as God.

Jesus Himself called God as *"God the Father (John 6:27)," "Our Father who is in Heaven (Matthew 6:9)," "the Holy Father (John 17:11),"* and *"My Father (John 20:17),"* teaching His disciples repeatedly to ensure that they would take

His teaching to their hearts.

In Christianity, we become true believers by encountering and believing in Jesus Christ revealed in the gospel of the water and the Spirit, God His Father, and God the Holy Spirit. Christians must know who exactly is this God that they believe in.

Christians Believe in God as the Father of All Mankind

Christians believe in the Triune God as the fundamental Author of mankind—that is, they believe God to be both the source and the nurturer of life. God created mankind, and saves and nurtures the saints through His Church.

Because the God of Christianity created the whole universe and made human beings in His own image, He is the Father of all mankind. When a missionary preached the gospel to some native Americans for the first time, an old chief asked him, "Did you say that God is our Father?" The missionary replied earnestly, "Yes!" The chief then asked again, "Are you saying that God is also my Father then?" The missionary answered, "Certainly!" Suddenly, the chief's face turned bright, extended his hands, and said, "Then you and I are brothers!" In God the Father, all human beings are brothers and sisters physically. Their spiritual fraternity, on the other hand, is made complete when they believe in the gospel of the water and the Spirit.

True world peace is found only when people encounter and serve God the Creator who is the root of mankind. If human beings, remaining ignorant of God, seek after only the roots of their own ancestors and pursue chauvinistic nationalism, humanity will surely be self-destroyed by pride, covetousness, jealousy, hatred, conflict, and war. As such, we must all become the spiritual children of God by faith within the gospel of the water and the Spirit that God has given us.

It is God the Father who gives us warm morning sun lights, beautiful sunsets, the four seasons, and the day and night. And it is He who feeds and nurtures all life forms, both mankind and animals, by bringing down rain and snow and giving us the abundant fruits of the earth. This is why Psalm 100:3 sings, *"Know that the LORD, He is God; It is He who has made us, and not we ourselves; We are His people and the sheep of His pasture."*

Because God knows how our bodies function, He feeds us with the appropriate products for each of the four seasons. For example, because we sweat a lot from the heat of summer, God gives us fresh and juicy fruits such as peaches, watermelons, tomatoes, grapes, and others.

In particular, we cannot help but be amazed by the wonderful inner-workings of our own bodies. Now it is well known that the life of human beings is found in their blood, but this was already written in the Scripture over 3,500 years ago (Leviticus 17:11). This blood circulates inside our bodies for over 675 km in a single day. If we were to walk any distance over 40 km in a day without resting, we would all be exhausted in no time. Yet our hearts circulate blood for over 675 km in just a single day, without any rest at all for 365 days a year. We switch off lights when we go to sleep, but our hearts are never switched off. Who, then, is pumping these hearts? It is the Father of life who works in the innermost mysteries of life that we do not know.

The air that human beings breathe, the water that they drink, and the food that they eat have all been given by God clearly. This is why Jacob, a man of faith, said, *"The God who has fed me all my life long to this day (Genesis 48:15)."* Also, to the ungrateful people of Israel, Isaiah said, *"Hear, O heavens, and give ear, O earth! For the LORD has spoken: 'I have nourished and brought up children, And they have rebelled against Me; The ox knows its owner And the donkey its master's crib; But Israel does not know, My people do not consider (Isaiah 1:2-3).'"*

As such, we must realize that it is God who feeds and nourishes our souls. God is the nurturer and the Father of all mankind.

We Must Recognize God as the One Who Has Saved Us from the Sins of the World

The love of God that has saved us from our sins is unlimited and eternal. But the history of mankind changes, and its religions also change countless times. But the love of God is never-changing, yesterday, today, and tomorrow.

People's carnal love cannot last forever. Emotionally stirred, we only think that it is love, but it changes in no time. What changes constantly is none other than emotion. The carnal love of human beings is always selfish and self-centered.

But the truthful love of God is absolute, sacrificial, and eternal. This is why the Bible tells us that God loved the world so much that He sent His only begotten Son. This is how He has saved us from the sins of the world. As such, Romans 5:8 says, *"But God demonstrates His own love toward us, in that while we were still sinners, Christ died for us.";* John 3:16 says, *"For God so loved the world that He gave His only begotten Son, that whoever believes in Him should not perish but have everlasting life.";* and 1 John 4:10 says, *"In this is love, not that we loved God, but that He loved us and sent His Son to be the propitiation for our sins."* We must believe in God, but we must also be saved from all our sins and receive eternal life by believing in the gospel of the water and the Spirit.

God Hears Our Prayers

The paternal relationship between a father and a child is a relationship where blood and flesh are shared. Likewise, those who believe in God become His children by believing in the baptism of Jesus Christ and His blood as the gospel of the remission of sin. This is how they can live in one house altogether. While we are on this earth, none other than God's Church is the house of the saints, and when we leave this world behind, our house is the eternal Kingdom of Heaven.

The blessing of calling God as our own Father and being saved from all our sins is made possible only within the faith that believes in the gospel of the water and the Spirit. Romans 8:15 thus says, *"For you did not receive the spirit of bondage again to fear, but you received the Spirit of adoption by whom we cry out, 'Abba, Father.'"* This is a marvelous fact, and absolutely true! The true gospel of the water and the Spirit is the gospel that forgives everyone from all sins. It is by faith, therefore, that we can be forgiven of all sins.

And the Holy Spirit can come to only those who have been forgiven of all their sins by believing in the gospel of the water and the Spirit. And only those who have received the Holy Spirit can become His sons and daughters. And by their faith in the Lord, they can all receive whatever they ask God in the name of Jesus Christ. John 16:23 therefore states, *"Most assuredly, I say to you, whatever you ask the Father in My name He will give you."*

God is the Father who, no matter how much His believers continue to call upon His name, is neither annoyed nor reproachful (James 1:5).

We Must Believe in God as the One Who Would Give Us Our Inheritance

Those who believe in the gospel of the water and the Spirit given by the Lord have become His adopted sons and daughters. As Romans 8:15 states, *"For you did not receive the spirit of bondage again to fear, but you received the Spirit of adoption by whom we cry out, 'Abba, Father.'"*

And if they have become God's sons and daughters, then this means that they will most certainly enjoy their inheritance of the afterlife. As Romans 8:17-18 says, *"And if children, then heirs—heirs of God and joint heirs with Christ, if indeed we suffer with Him, that we may also be glorified together. For I consider that the sufferings of this present time are not worthy to be compared with the glory which shall be revealed in us."* Here, the word *"heirs"* is emphasized three times, meaning those who would succeed God—that is, His own inheritors.

Galatians 4:7 also states, *"Therefore you are no longer a slave but a son, and if a son, then an heir of God through Christ."* The phrase, *"joint heirs with Christ,"* tells us that we are the ones who will inherit everything that the God of Christianity has. By ourselves, we cannot even dare to enter the Kingdom of Heaven without the faith that believes in the gospel of the water and the Spirit. But by believing in the baptism and blood of God's only begotten Son, we can receive the remission of our sins, and then enter the Kingdom of Heaven. John 6:39 states, *"This is the will of the Father who sent Me, that of all He has given Me I should lose nothing, but should raise it up at the last day."*

"I believe in ..."
(John 1:12-13)

The confession of the faith in the Apostles' Creed is the declaration of the Apostles' faith that affirms how exactly they believe in God. As such, this faith must begin with the confession, "I believe in God the Father Almighty."

The reason for doing so is because we want to have the faith that God wants from us. Leading the life of faith is for each individual to believe in the Triune God, for faith begins by thus knowing and believing in God the Almighty. This faith reflects the desire to have the faith that God wants from us. When we believe in God, it is impossible for us to reach the conclusion that God created the universe by engaging in our own deductive thinking or experiments. We reach this conclusion only by believing the Word of God the Creator.

When it comes to the issues that we cannot directly authenticate and prove by ourselves, we can only accept the authoritative Word. The Word of the Scriptures is the authoritative truth. The prophets and the Apostles are the Bible writers who were inspired by the Holy Spirit. Jesus is God the Savior who healed people from their incurable illnesses and raised even the dead to live again. Inspired by God, the prophets wrote God's Word from the account of God's creation of the universe to His salvation through His Son Jesus. And by believing in their writings as they are, we can ascertain the truthfulness of His Word, and meet the God of truth.

In Christianity, people who really believe in Jesus as the Savior believe in the gospel of the water and the Spirit that saves them from all their sins. Because the protagonist of this gospel is Jesus, we take what Jesus said as ours by believing in His Word. We must all believe in the Word of the God of Christianity, for we need the Savior as we were all born as sinners from our very birth. Sinners can be saved when they believe in the gospel Word of the water and the Spirit that Jesus has given them. This is the truth that God has bestowed on mankind. ⌧

PART

II

II. CONFESSION OF FAITH IN GOD THE SON

"I believe in Jesus Christ, His only Son our Lord,
who was conceived by the Holy Ghost,
born of the Virgin Mary,
suffered under Pontius Pilate, was crucified,
died, and was buried;
He descended into hell;
The third day He rose again from the dead;
He ascended into heaven, and sitteth on the right hand of God the Father Almighty; from thence
He shall come to judge the quick and the dead."

Jesus Christ
(Ιησοῦ Χριστου)

The name Jesus, "Ιησους (*iesous*)" in Greek, is originated from Hebrew name ישוע (*yeh-ho-shoo'-ah*), meaning "Jehovah is salvation."

Christ is משיח in Hebrew and Χριστός in Greek, meaning "the anointed one." The name Christ is the New Testament's appellation for the Old Testament's Messiah. The expression "ὁ Χριστός *(ho khris-tos)*" that frequently appears in the Four Gospel is the word "Christ" preceded by the definite article "the," telling us that Jesus is the absolute God Himself. God the Father, in other words, sent His own Son to deliver everyone living in this world from all sins.

Strictly speaking, these two names of "Jesus" and "Christ" are not actually interchangeable. The name "Jesus" is the name of the Savior who came as the Interceder of mankind, as the peacemaker between God and human beings. But the name "Christ" means "the anointed one," originating from the traditions of the ancient Middle East region—that is, from the ritual of distinguishing those chosen to bear the responsibilities of high positions by anointing them.

For the people of Israel in the Old Testament's time, this tradition was originated from God's own command. They anointed prophets, priests, and kings (1 Kings 19:16, Psalm 133:2). This was the ritual that publicly affirmed before everyone the fact that those chosen by God were fit for the duties of each. Such symbolic rituals of the Old Testament, however, were effective only for the certain period of duration when these people entrusted with such duties were alive, and even so their capacity to fulfill their duties was also imperfect. These facts implied that the Israelites could not but wait for the coming of the perfect One who would be anointed by God Himself.

In such a context, there was the birth of One who would be especially anointed by the Holy Spirit to fulfill the righteousness of God (Matthew 3:15-17, Mark 1:10-11, Luke 3:21-22). Jesus Himself testified on this, *"The Spirit of the LORD is upon Me, Because He has anointed Me…" (Luke 4:18;* see also *Isaiah 61:1).* Thus, the name "Christ" means "the anointed One" who saves His people from sin. Contained in the name of Christ are not only His duties as the Redeemer and Interceder, but also His authority and power manifested by His perfect fulfillment of these duties.

1. Christ's Attributes

Christ already existed even before the creation (Ephesians 1:4). Explaining the will that God had even before the creation, Paul said, *"In the dispensation of the fullness of the times He might gather together in one all things in Christ, both which are in heaven and which are on earth—in Him" (Ephesians 1:10).*

To fulfill His will, God sent His only begotten Son, whom He had promised and who would be anointed, to this earth. The family lineage of this Son of God is shown in more detail in the covenant that God established with Abraham—that is, He would come as one of the descendants of Abraham, and all the nations would be blessed because of Him (Genesis 22:17-19). This was God's promise.

Jacob, while blessing his sons in his dying hour, also said that the Messiah would come as a descendant of Judah (Genesis 49:10). The prophets of the latter times revealed the attributes and ministries of the Messiah in even more detail. According to Isaiah 53, it was prophesied that Christ would take the sins of His people upon Himself, be crucified, suffer at the hands of people and be abandoned by them, and ultimately die and be buried.

(1) The Divine Nature of Jesus Christ: Jesus Christ has not only existed even before the creation, but He has existed as the eternal and true God. Furthermore, even though He came to this earth in the flesh of a man, He has continued to be God Himself (John 1:1, 14). As Romans 9:5 states, *"[He] who is* *over all, the eternally blessed God."*

The confession of God's Church about the divine nature of Jesus Christ is not a man-made confession, for this is founded on the very revelation of God Himself (Matthew 16:17). In addition, all the truths of the Bible describe the divine nature of Christ explicitly, not ambiguously (Micah 5:2; Isaiah 9:6). In the New Testament, the true divinity of Christ the Savior is often solemnly declared by Christ Himself. Peter also confessed to Jesus, *"You are the Christ, the Son of the living God"* (*Matthew 16:16;* see also Mark 8:29 and Luke 9:20).

Furthermore, Paul also said, *"[Christ Jesus] who, "being in the form of God, did not consider it robbery to be equal with God" (Philippians 2:6).* John, while praising Christ, also confessed, *"And we know that the Son of God has come and has given us an understanding, that we may know Him who is true; and we are in Him who is true, in His Son Jesus Christ. This is the true God and eternal life" (1 John 5:20).* When Caiaphas the High Priest asked Jesus, *"Tell us if You are the Christ, the Son of God,"* Jesus answered him, *"It is as you said" (Matthew 26:63-64;* see also Mark 15:2).

On other occasions, Jesus also said that He and God the Father were one (John 10:30), and that He had existed before Abraham (John 8:58). Christ, moreover, mentioned His role as the High Priest and the glory that He has shared with the Father even before the creation (John 17:5). In addition, when Christ forgave people of their sins or healed them from their illnesses, as well as when He admonished His disciples to believe in Him, all these things were contingent upon their recognition of His divinity.

Jesus Christ is the Second Person of the Triune God who worked as the Son of God (Matthew 16:16; 26:63-64).

According to the angel that visited Mary, the Son whom Mary would give birth would be called as the Holy Son of God (Luke 1:35). Right after Jesus was baptized by John, a voice came from Heaven and testified, *"This is My beloved Son, in whom I am well pleased"* (*Matthew 3:17;* see also Mark 1:11 and Luke 3:22).

This meant that His baptism was not simply a ritual, but the one approved by God the Father. It refers to the baptism that Jesus received to take all the sins of mankind upon Himself. This is how He fulfilled all the righteousness of God (Matthew 3:15). Just before Jesus was baptized, He said to John, *"Permit it to be so now* [that is, baptize Me], *for thus it is fitting for us to fulfill all righteousness" (Matthew 3:15).* The Bible declares that Jesus Christ has the same particular power as the Father (John 5:26). The Apostle Paul calls Christ as God's *"own Son" (Romans 8:32).* And John says that Christ was *"the Word* [who] *was with God" (John 1:1).* He also describes Him as God's only begotten Son (John 1:14, 3:16; see also 5:18, where Jesus Himself called God as His own Father.)

(2) The Human Nature of Jesus Christ: Christ's human nature is also emphasized in the New Testament. The eternal Son of God was born *"in the likeness of men" (Philippians 2:7-8).* He was called *"the Man Christ Jesus" (1 Timothy 2:5).* Even though He was God Himself, He incarnated into a man and dwelt among us (John 1:14). In consequence, He was baptized by John the Baptist. He lived among people as a man, and He shared in their happiness, joy and sadness. And He also ate the same food that they ate. He was a man not only in His appearance, but in His character. Like others, He was also a descendant of Adam (the family lineage of Luke 3:38). And He was born of a woman (Luke 2:6-7; Matthew 1:18-25, and

Galatians 4:4). Among His forefathers were Abraham and David (Matthew 1:1).

Even though Jesus Himself had no sin, He nonetheless came to this earth in the flesh of a man weakened by sins. In other words, Christ came "in the likeness of sinful flesh," and by being baptized by John, He fulfilled all the righteousness of God (John 19:30). Although He shouldered our sins with His baptism and suffered, He was not differentiated from others (Isaiah 53:2-3).

However, although Christ had the same human nature as us, He never surrendered to the temptation of sin. According to the author of the Book of Hebrews, Christ was *"in all points tempted as we are, yet without sin" (Hebrew 4:15).* Jesus bore sins only because He took the sins of the world upon Himself by being baptized by John, and this is why He was crucified for the sake of sinners. Referring to Christ, Hebrews 7:26 states, *"For such a High Priest was fitting for us, who is holy, harmless, undefiled, separate from sinners."*

Christ's Three Duties

There were three kinds of persons who were anointed by oil in the Old Testament age: the prophets, the priests, and the kings (1 Kings 19:16; Exodus 40:13-15; 2 Kings 9:3).

Christ is the Prophet and the Teacher anointed by the Holy Spirit. And He is also the heavenly High Priest. The concepts of the many roles that Christ played are all biblically sound. Deuteronomy 18:15 states, *"The LORD your God will raise up for you a Prophet"* (see also verse 18). In Psalm 110:4, Jehovah called Christ by saying, *"You are a priest forever."* Zechariah 6:12-13 reveals the Kinghood of Christ by stating that "the Man whose name is the BRANCH" would "bear the glory" and "sit and rule on His throne." These three duties of Christ were all fulfilled when Christ came to this earth, shouldered all the sins of the world by being baptized by John, was crucified and shed His blood on the Cross, and rose again from the dead.

A. Prophet: Like the prophets of the Old Testament, Christ fulfilled His prophetic role by revealing the will of God and implementing God's Word to His people. But Christ was not merely a simple prophet or messenger. He was the greatest Prophet for mankind. His Word was the complete and perfect Word of God that no prophet can ever add to or subtract from. This is because all the treasures of wisdom and knowledge are hidden in Him (Colossians 2:3). It is also because He is *"the only begotten Son, who is in the bosom of the Father" (John 1:18).*

Christ's message was made sufficient when He had completed His mission: To fulfill all righteousness of God, Jesus was baptized by John, and shed His blood on the Cross; And He calls every sinner to be remitted of all his/her sins within the righteousness He had completed. Therefore, such true knowledge of God and teachings on salvation cannot be attained without believing in the baptism of Christ and the blood of the Cross. Those who do not believe are condemned already, because they have not believed in the name of the only begotten Son of God, and thus remain sinful (John 3:18). They cannot find the way of eternal life, either. Because Christ's sermons had power and authority as the Prophet, they led the listeners to obey His Word.

B. High Priest: In Psalm 110:4, speaking to His anointed One, God said, *"You are a priest forever According to the order of Melchizedek."* This means that Christ is the High Priest not from the order of Aaron, but He is the High Priest as a result of Jehovah's special and singular calling and appointment. The priests of the Old Testament, who had served in the Tabernacle or the Temple, were the foreshadowers of this Christ to come, presaging Christ as the perfect and eternal High Priest. He works as the perfect High Priest, *"For Christ has not entered the holy places made with hands, which are copies of the true, but into heaven itself, now to appear in the presence of God for us" (Hebrews 9:24).*

There are three dimensions to Christ's ministry as the High Priest.

First, He had offered Himself as the sacrifice for our sins forever. Jesus Christ, in other words, had redeemed all mankind from destruction with His baptism and bloodshed. He has completed God's righteousness by having obtained eternal redemption for us. Christ's sacrifice of atonement had been foretold and known for thousands years through the sacrificial system under the old sacrificial rituals of the laying on of hands. In particular, this was typically revealed through the laying of hands on the head of the Passover lamb and its bloodshed.

In contrast to the sacrificial offerings of Aaron and other priests of the Old Testament, which were symbolic and repetitive, Christ came to this earth only once, and by taking the sins of the world upon Himself through His baptism received from John and dying on the Cross, He fulfilled all the righteousness of God once and for all. This is why He was baptized and gave all the perfect sacrificial offerings on the Cross. Christ, as Hebrew 9:26 states, *"once at the end of the ages... has appeared to put away sin by the sacrifice of Himself."*

He is the Lamb of God who shouldered the sins of the world with His baptism and carried them to the Cross

(Matthew 3:13-17). Christ reveals to us that He Himself was sacrificed as "our own Passover Lamb." By sacrificing Himself for the sins of mankind, He paid the price of redemption to God for the sake of His people. As Hebrew 9:28 states, *"Christ was offered once to bear the sins of many."* He did not enter by means of the blood of goats and calves; but he entered the Most Holy Place once for all by His own blood, having obtained eternal redemption (Hebrews 9:12). This was achieved by accepting His baptism and the Cross. He did like the High Priests of the Old Testament, who, on the Day of Atonement, had entered the Most Holy with the blood of sacrifice.

Likewise, by being baptized in His body, Christ also accepted the sins of the world passed onto Him, and ascended to Heaven after having atoned all the sins of the world with the blood of the Cross, thereby entering the Sanctuary of Heaven with His own blood of sacrifice. By doing so, Christ has saved all those who believe in His baptism and blood from their guilt and curses.

Above all, for the salvation of His people from their sins, Christ was able to achieve all His works, including being baptized by John and shedding His blood on the Cross. With His "voluntary obedience"—that is, by being baptized—Christ bore the sins of His people, and with His "active obedience"—that is, by carrying the sins of the world to the Cross and being crucified—He fulfilled the righteousness of God perfectly. It is when we believe in this that we attain our eligibility for salvation. By coming to this earth and giving up His body as the sacrifice for all mankind, Christ fulfilled all the righteous works of God. By doing so, He has saved His people who, because of the corruption of Adam, had become sinners, from all their sins. It is by this work that Christ fulfilled God's righteous plan perfectly. By giving His baptism and blood to

His people, He enabled them to receive the righteousness of God.

The second aspect to the priestly ministry of Christ is prayer. He not only enables mankind simply to approach God, but more so, He enables them to go boldly to the throne of grace (Hebrews 4:16; see also 10:19). Christ not only teaches how to pray (Luke 11:1-4; Matthew 6:9-13), but He also guarantees before God the prayers of whoever prays truthfully in His name, and by imploring God based on His works, He makes it possible that his/her prayers would be answered. Christ Himself prays for His people, and He works as the Interceder who, for their sake, pleads on their behalf and defends them before God.

Such works were already done when Christ was ministering on this earth (Luke 22:32; 23:34; John 17), and they continue to be fulfilled now, even after He was exalted and entered the Sanctuary of Heaven to sit at the right hand of God the Father (Romans 8:34). Christ understood perfectly all the sufferings and sadness of human beings, knew their needs well, and approached such needs with a compassionate and merciful heart. As Hebrew 4:15 states, *"For we do not have a High Priest who cannot sympathize with our weaknesses, but was in all points tempted as we are, yet without sin."* His prayers reflect His profound understanding of the needs of mankind.

The third dimension to Christ's priestly ministry is asking for the blessings of His people. In the Old Testament, one of the priests' duties was to lay their hands on their people and bless them. God promised that when the priests blessed the descendants of Israel in the name of Jehovah, He would indeed give them His blessings (Numbers 6:22-27). Likewise, when Christ was ministering on this earth, His very existence itself was already a blessing, and when He ascended to Heaven, He also raised His hands and blessed His disciples (Luke 24:50-51). Furthermore, even now He blesses His people with every spiritual blessing of Heaven (Ephesians 1:3). Through His Spirit, He bestows the gifts of Heaven on them, and brings them the never-ending showers of blessings.

Like this, Christ is God Himself for whom there can be no other comparison, for Christ alone could become the sacrifice of atonement, and, standing at the side of His people, He alone could fulfill the Law perfectly. As such, only Christ is the Interceder who brings us the blessings of Heaven. Now, if there are people who do not believe in His priestly ministry, they will certainly not be able to find any other priest who can atone for their sins. Because they cannot find any interceder who is with God, they will, far from receiving the blessings of Heaven, all face their eternal condemnation instead.

C. King: Christ was also anointed as the King for His duties, like the Old Testament's kings. But He is not like the preceding kings, whose glory and power were attained by force. Rather, Christ was anointed as the eternal King, and as the King who would reign with infinite power, justice and truth.

John draws attention to the fact that Christ's Kingdom *"is not of this world" (John 18:36).* Paul, on the other hand, teaches that the Kingdom of God is constituted only of *"righteousness and peace and joy in the Holy Spirit" (Romans 14:17).* The author of Hebrews says that this King rules with His Word: *"For the word of God is living and powerful, and sharper than any two-edged sword, piercing even to the division of soul and spirit, and of joints and marrow, and is a discerner of the thoughts and intents of the heart" (Hebrews 4:12).* Moreover, the sovereign Kinghood of Christ is not limited to the Jewish nation. Christ is the Head of the Church, the congregation of His believers (Ephesians 4:15).

This church has been redeemed from the dominion of the Devil, and has been built with the blood of Christ. His church is led by the Holy Spirit, and it belongs to Christ forever. As the King, Christ protects His Church from any danger. He does not allow any forces, no matter what they may be, to ever overcome the church. Even if such forces were the gates of Hades (hell), they cannot prevail against the church (Matthew 16:18).

In addition, His rule is merciful and perfect. Through such rule, He makes His people submit to His authority and obey His words. Furthermore, even those who do not recognize His sovereignty cannot escape from the reign of Christ, for God the Father has enabled the Son to rule over the entire universe. The Father has given Christ all authority. Jesus therefore says, *"All authority has been given to Me in heaven and on earth" (Matthew 28:18).* Paul writes that the triumphant Christ stripped the evil angels of their authority (Colossians 2:15). The Apostle John says Christ is *"the ruler over the kings of the earth" (Revelation 1:5).*

The sovereign authority of Christ may seem to be ignored on this earth, and His glory may appear to be blasphemed, insulted, and hidden by His evil enemies (Psalm 89:51). But His majesty continues to shine in Heaven as the King of kings and the Lord of lords (Revelation 19:16). In the end, Christ will ultimately come back in the clouds, and He will give honor to those who have believed and shame to those who have rejected Him (Matthew 25:31-46). When this time comes, the reign of Christ will be manifested through His righteousness everywhere in Heaven and on earth (2 Peter 3:13, Revelation 21).

In the New Testament, Christ was the Prophet, and at the

same time He was the High Priest and the King. When Christ spoke as a Prophet, His teachings were accompanied with His authority as the King (Luke 4:32). When Christ admitted to Pilate that He was indeed a King, He also said that He came to this world as a Prophet to testify the truth (John 18:37). When Christ performed miracles, His sovereign authority was revealed, such miracles were secured by His prophetic teachings, and these miracles were bestowed by His priestly mercy (Matthew 8:17).

Sermon on the Holy Son 1

Who Is Jesus Christ?

Why Did Jesus Come to This World?

Jesus came through the body of a virgin.

Reason: To save human beings from sin, He had to come in their flesh.

In what form did He come?

He came in a form that had nothing to be desired of.

Jesus came to the nation of Israel, as a man, and through the body of the Virgin Mary engaged to Joseph, for He came to fulfill the Word of prophecy for the sake of mankind. Christ came to become the light for this dark world.

He came to become and work as the Interceder between God and mankind. After being baptized by John and while thus shouldering the sins of the world, He was crucified and shed His blood on the Cross. As such, He came to give the remission of sin and life to those who believe.

Christ came to enable us to enter the Kingdom of Heaven by believing in His baptism of the cleansing of sin and the blood of the Cross, and to allow us to avoid the fiery hell.

This world had been a dark and hopeless world. Before Christ came to this world, there was no light of true salvation, but worse, it was locked in pitch-black darkness. To such a world as this, Jesus came. Why did Jesus come? He came to shine the light of salvation to this world.

Actually, Jesus was not born in December. Rather, He was

born in a season when the fields of Israel were filled with green grass, when shepherds tended their sheep out in the open field and let them graze there (Luke 2:8). This verifies the fact that His actual birthday was not December 25.

Why, then, do we celebrate Christmas on this cold day of December 25? This was because from the mid 4th century A.D., the Western Church set this day of December 25 as the birthday of Jesus to prevent the spread of the pagan worship of a sun god. But this day was actually a day of worshipping the sun god. Aiming to inhibit the participation in this pagan celebration and to prevent the adulteration of Christians' faith, the same day of pagan festivity was proclaimed as the birthday of Jesus, in a kind of strategy akin to fighting fire with fire.

We are not sure exactly when Jesus' birthday is, but we do know for certain that the Son of God came to save the entire mankind, and we therefore set aside a day of the year to celebrate His coming, regardless of whether or not December 25 had actually been a day of pagan celebration. Because the whole world celebrates the day when Jesus was born to save us from our sins, we set a day, remember it, and thank and praise Him.

When Jesus came to this earth, all the people of this world had been deceived by the Devil, their hearts were weighed down by their sins, and they truly did not know the way of receiving eternal life. This is why God the Father sent His Son Jesus to save the people of the world from all their sins.

The name Jesus is the name of the Savior, meaning He who will save His people from their sins. This Jesus came to this world. By bearing the sins of the world with His baptism, Jesus was condemned on the Cross and has thereby blotted out all these sins.

Was Jesus God?

Yes. Jesus was God Himself in His essence. Jesus is the very One who created the whole universe with the Word of His mouth. This world, in fact, was created by God. John 1:3 says, "All things were made through Him, and without Him nothing was made that was made." Jesus was God Himself who came to save sinners. Jesus created this world and the whole universe in the beginning. When Jesus said, "let there be light," then there was light. When He said, "let there be the sun," then the sun came into existence. It is by this command of Jesus, "let there be," that all the grasses, trees, the sea, the sky, and even mankind itself came into existence. Jesus is God who created all these things in the beginning (Genesis 1:3-15).

He was fundamentally the God of creation. All things were made through Him, and there was nothing that was made without Him. Why, then, did He come to this earth incarnated in the flesh of a man?

He came to save all the sinners of this world from all their sins. The reason that God came to mankind was to shine the true light to each and every one of sinner and thereby saving them all from their sins.

John 1:9-12 states, *"That was the true Light which gives light to every man coming into the world. He was in the world, and the world was made through Him, and the world did not know Him. He came to His own, and His own did not receive Him. But as many as received Him, to them He gave the right to become children of God, to those who believe in His name."*

The Son of God came to blot out all the sins that we have inherited from Adam, the father of mankind, and to drive away darkness from this world. His name is Jesus Christ, and Jesus Christ is the Son of God the Father.

Why Did People Not Receive Jesus into Their Hearts?

Because He has saved sinners from their sins by coming as a lowly man.

Because people did not cast aside their own faith and their own thoughts.

Because they did not realize that they had been created by God.

Because they did not know that they are bound to hell because they have been sinners from the very moment of their birth.

Because people did not know that Jesus is the Savior.

Because they were ignorant of the truth.

Because they did not recognize the Savior who is God Himself.

Because they did not respond to the gospel of the water and the Spirit.

Because they did not know Jesus, who is the way and the truth.

Jesus was born in Bethlehem, a small, rural town in Israel.

Why was Jesus born in this world? He came to us to save those who are ill-treated in this world and who are truly living lowly lives in this world. Jesus came to save those who are tormented by their sins, who want to enter the Kingdom of Heaven, and who want to be clothed in God's grace. This is why Jesus was born in a manger.

However, when Jesus came to this world in the likeness of human beings, the people of Israel did not recognize Him as God and the Messiah. They did not realize that He was the Son of God, the very Creator God who made the whole universe and everything in it. This is why the people of Israel did not receive Him. This is true even now. Many people in this world still do not know that Jesus is the God of creation and the Savior who has saved human beings from all their sins.

Isaiah wrote that when God looked down from Heaven, *"He saw that there was no man, and wondered that there was no intercessor [Savior]" (Isaiah 59:16).* God Himself had to come up with salvation, and He Himself had to come to this earth and make us sinless—that is, make the sinful sinless. Coming to this earth, to bring down the wall that had sprung up in our relationship with God the Father as a result of our sins and separated us from Him, He took all the sins of mankind upon Himself with His baptism and bore the condemnation of all these sins of mankind by being crucified and shedding His blood on the Cross. He has thereby saved those who believe.

No matter how human beings have no righteousness of their own, no matter how insufficient and weak they are, and no matter how many sins they have committed, if they only realize that Jesus fulfilled all righteousness by taking upon their sins with His baptism and shedding His blood on the Cross, and if they accept this truth into their hearts, they can all be saved from all their sins.

As such, there is only one true Savior in this world, and this Savior is only Jesus. The name of Jesus itself means "He who will save His people from their sins" (Matthew 1:21).

By doing what can we enter Heaven? Can we enter Heaven by doing good deeds?

No!

Being born into this world, can we live without ever sinning?

No!

It is impossible for us not to ever sin. We cannot help but sin for the rest of our lives until our own demise. Can people enter Heaven when they have a sin as small as a penny?

No!

Is there anyone in this world, then, who can enter Heaven by his own strength?

No!

By whom can we then enter Heaven?

We can enter Heaven by believing in the gospel of the water and the Spirit given by Jesus Christ.

"For He will save His people from their sins" (Matthew 1:21). God made us, and when we fell into sin, He became a man and came to this earth to make our sins disappear. The One who thus came to this earth, was baptized, and died on the Cross is none other than Jesus.

When We Believe in Jesus, How Can We Receive Him Truly?

John 1:12 says, *"But as many as received Him, to them He gave the right to become children of God, to those who believe in His name."* To those who believe that Jesus has become their Savior and blotted out all their sins, He has given them the right to become God's children. Have you received the gospel of the water and the Spirit?

What is receiving the truth? One can receive the truth only when he/she knows the truth of the water and the Spirit. When someone is knocking on the door, we open the door only slightly and first ask who it is, and if it is someone whom we know, we then open the door fully and ask him/her to come in. This is receiving.

Although we have not actually met Jesus face to face, we still believe that He accepted all our sins passed onto Him by being baptized at the Jordan River. I thank God for this truth. I may not be able to extend any loan guarantees, but what I can guarantee definitely is the Word that we can enter the Kingdom of God if we only believe in the gospel of the water and the Spirit. That you are made sinless is, in itself, becoming God's children. That you receive eternal life by faith is the truth.

The faith that receives the blessings of Heaven is the faith in the gospel of the water and the Spirit given by God. This means believing not only that Jesus bore all your sins with His baptism, but also that He came to this earth and took away once and for all every sin that you would commit for the rest of your lives and until the end of the world. Jesus, whom I believe, has made us sinless all at once by taking away our sins of the world once and for all.

"Believe." Faith is a beautiful word. "Receive." I accepted the truth that Jesus is my Savior into my heart. I am no better than anyone else. Yet even so, the reason why I can speak in confidence and at times even be proud is because of my faith in the gospel of the water and the Spirit.

By all means, I hope that you would all know and believe in the gospel of the water and the Spirit. It is only when we know the truth of the water and the Spirit and believe in it that we can finally be born again, become sinless, and thereby also become God's children.

Do you know and believe in the truth that Jesus took all your sins upon Himself when He was baptized at the Jordan River? Jesus accepted the condemnation of all the sins that you have committed throughout your entire lifetime and was vicariously punished on the Cross in your place. He then arose from the dead in three days and now sits at the right hand of the throne of God the Father. Even now, our God is alive.

John 1:9 says, *"That was the true Light which gives light*

to every man coming into the world." This Light is the Light of Jesus who took upon the sins of the world by being baptized by John and dying on the Cross. All that we have to do is just receive this true Light shone by our Lord. We must accept into our hearts the truth that Jesus came as the Savior of us the sinners. We must believe that Jesus bore all our sins by being baptized at the Jordan River. When we believe that He thus fulfilled all the righteousness of God, we can then be saved from all our sins.

In our flesh, we are unable to believe in Jesus. But in our hearts, we can know the righteousness of God, believe in it, and thereby receive it. Once, we had been in pitch-black darkness. That this darkness is removed by the true Light shinning in our hearts means the removal of our sins from our hearts by our faith in the Word of truth. This true Light is the Word of the truth through which we have been born again of water and the Spirit, and the true Light gives us light because we have believed in and accepted into our hearts the baptism that Jesus received from John and His bloodshed on the Cross.

It is appointed for men to be born once and die once. The Bible tells us that our lifetime is about 70 years, or 80 if we are strong (Psalm 90:10). Every human being goes through the trials of life, and, at its end, must stand before the Lord. How pitiful would it be if we were to die without knowing the truth of the water and the Spirit? Even if we were to live beyond 80, we must all die once at some point. But we do not simply cease to exist after dying. Judgment follows our death. Whether we are welcomed into Heaven or cast into hell is determined by whether we have the faith that believes in the water and the blood of Jesus Christ. While we are still living on this earth, we must therefore receive the blessing of believing in Jesus' baptism and accepting it into our hearts.

Some people say, "I am not someone who can believe in Jesus. Why? Because I was born as a natural sinner, whose propensity to sin is boundless." But even these people need not worry. Their sins, too, were all passed onto Jesus through His baptism and blood, and, as such, all that they have to do is just entrust everything to Him by believing in this Word. I beseech you to leave all your weaknesses and flaws of your hearts, which you cannot ever control on your own, at the feet of God, for if you would only entrust all your sins to Him, our Lord, being the Almighty God that He is, has already solved all the problems of your sins through His baptism and blood.

While we live in this world, we must always believe in the gospel of the water and the Spirit in our hearts. We must live with our faith always prepared to enter Heaven. And when we believe in the gospel of the water and the Spirit given by Jesus, we are then born again. When you do so, you should realize, the blessings of God are then spread throughout the entire world through none other than yourselves.

When we believe in gospel of the water and the Spirit given by God, He then protects us. We must receive Jesus by believing that He has become our Savior. And let us also thank Him for being our Savior.

We Must Know and Believe in Jesus Who Is Both Divine and Human (John 1:14)

The Apostles believed in the Son of God our Lord as the Savior.

The name Jesus means "the Savior," and the name Christ means "the anointed One." This means that Jesus fulfilled His role as the Prophet, that He is the King of kings, and, therefore,

He also fulfilled the role of the High Priest of the Kingdom of Heaven.

First of all, the Old Testament clearly specifies that the Christ to come is God Himself. A representative passage of this is found in Isaiah 9:6, which states, *"Unto us a Child is born, Unto us a Son is given; And the government will be upon His shoulder. And His name will be called Wonderful, Counselor, Mighty God, Everlasting Father, Prince of Peace."*

In addition, our Lord's own Word bears witness to this truth. To show just a couple of examples, Matthew 5:17 says, *"Do not think that I came to destroy the Law or the Prophets. I did not come to destroy but to fulfill."* No one else but the Savior God Himself alone can fulfill the Law. Also, in Matthew 9:6, Jesus said, *"But that you may know that the Son of Man has power on earth to forgive sins."*

Paul said in Philippians 2:5-6, *"Let this mind be in you which was also in Christ Jesus, who, being in the form of God, did not consider it robbery to be equal with God,"* and in Colossians 2:9, he said, *"For in Him dwells all the fullness of the Godhead bodily."*

Above all, the signs that Jesus performed while on this earth clearly show us that He is God. With only five loaves and two fish, He fed over 5,000 people, not counting women and children. On another occasion, He fed 4,000 people with just 7 loaves and 2 fish. Jesus also brought down winds with His rebuke. He walked on water, and delivered Peter who sank into water. Matthew 11:5 states, *"The blind see and the lame walk; the lepers are cleansed and the deaf hear; the dead are raised up."* All these things cannot be done by mere mortals, but they can be accomplished only by God. As such, Christ is clearly the living God and the Savior.

What Is the Meaning of the Baptism of Jesus? (Matthew 3:13-17)

We must believe that Jesus took the sins of the world upon Himself by being baptized by John the Baptist (Matthew 3:15). This baptism that Jesus received from John was to bear all the sins and iniquities of the sinners of this world. To realize this truth, we must first understand the meaning of the word "thus." This word "thus" is *"οὕτως (hoo'-tos)"* in Greek, and it means: 1) just in this way; 2) most fitting; and 3) there is no other way besides this. In other words, when Jesus came to this earth, He had to be baptized to accept the iniquities of sinners passed onto Him. If we do not believe so, our sins cannot be blotted out.

There are some people who have misunderstood the baptism of Jesus and mistakenly think that He was baptized to show us His humility. But this is not the case. The Word of the baptism of Jesus by John clearly bears witness to the truth that He was thus baptized in order to take upon all the sins of this world. Jesus could become the Savior of those who believe in Him because He, coming to this earth, accepted all the sins of this world passed onto His body in a single instance by receiving His baptism from John once and for all.

We cannot keep the Word of this truth of Jesus' baptism covered. Why? Because what Satan seeks after from sinners is to make them unable to know the Word of the baptism of Jesus, the most important aspect to mankind's remission of sin, and to incapacitate them from believing in it.

The Baptism of Jesus and the Blood of the Cross

The baptism that Jesus received from John is the work of

salvation through which He took the sins of mankind upon Himself. 1 John 5:4-6 tells us that Jesus' baptism is essential to our salvation. The reason why Jesus was baptized by John at the Jordan River is as the following.

That Jesus was baptized by John means that He fulfilled all the righteousness of God—that is, Jesus accepted all the sins of the world passed onto Him. When Jesus was baptized, His submersion in water tells us of His death, and His emersion from water tells us of His resurrection.

Jesus' baptism corresponds to the Word of the Old Testament found in Leviticus 16, where sacrificial offerings accepted the sins of the people of Israel with the laying on of hands. That this was done so had the same reason as to why Jesus was baptized by John the Baptist. It was the same reason for which Jesus commanded John, "You shall baptize me. Permit it be so. It is thus fitting for us to fulfill all righteousness." He said, "By my being baptized by you, and by your baptizing me, it is fitting to fulfill all righteousness."

What is it that everyone in this world desires and wishes the most? It is to become sinless in their hearts, in other words, to become the sinless children of God. The Bible tells us that for us to become so, we must believe in the Word that Jesus blotted out all the sins and iniquities of sinners by being baptized and shedding His blood on the Cross, and it tells us also that it is by thus believing that we can receive the righteousness of God. What, then, is all the righteousness of God? It is the Word telling us that as Jesus was baptized by John in this world, the iniquities of all sinners left them and were then passed onto the body of Jesus.

"For thus it is fitting for us to fulfill all righteousness (making all sinner righteous)." Jesus told John, in other words, that it is by being baptized by John that He would fulfill all the righteousness of God. To fulfill God's righteousness, Jesus had to be baptized and thereby accept all the sins and transgressions of sinners passed onto Him. On our part, what we must do is to believe in the baptism that Jesus received.

Jesus came to make all the sins and iniquities of sinners disappear. But those who do not believe in the truth are bound in their eternal sins forever and cannot escape from them at all. In the Bible, there is no way by which sinners can be saved from all the sins of the world but only to believe in the baptism of Jesus and the blood of the Cross written in the Word of God.

Even so, there are still many contrasting opinions as to the method with which Jesus Christ has blotted out the iniquities of sinners. Some people say that the Word of salvation from sin is only the Word of the blood of the Cross. But the Word of God written in the Scripture tells us that the Word of the baptism of Jesus is the most fitting for Him to make all the sins and transgressions of sinners disappear, for Jesus was thus baptized all at once and died on the Cross once and for all.

There are others who ask, "Is there no other method but this, that Jesus cleansed away the sins of the world by being baptized and shed His blood on the Cross?" But our Lord has told us clearly that the salvation of sinners comes only from His own providence, and that it is far from our place for us to question or blame the Word for how Jesus chose to save sinners.

There is a saying, "A taffy peddler does as he pleases." Likewise, when it comes to God's salvation of sinners from all their sins, if He Himself tells us that He has saved them through this method—that is, through the baptism of Jesus by John and His crucifixion—then all that we can do is just believe in what He tells us as it is. Who can then possibly object to the Word of God? People may refuse to believe in the Word of the baptism of Jesus received from John and of the blood of the Cross, and they may reject what God has told them, but they will certainly not be able to avoid hell.

Do you believe in the Word of God?

Sermon on the Holy Son 2

What Do the Old Testament's Laying on of Hands and the New Testament's Baptism Mean?

< Leviticus 1:3-4 >

"If his offering is a burnt sacrifice of the herd, let him offer a male without blemish; he shall offer it of his own free will at the door of the tabernacle of meeting before the LORD. Then he shall put his hand on the head of the burnt offering, and it will be accepted on his behalf to make atonement for him."

The Old Testament tells us that when the people of Israel gave to God their offering of the remission of sin, they had to make sure to bring an unblemished animal and to put their hands on its head. And it is also written that when priests, on their behalf, killed the animal, drew its blood, put the blood on the horns of the altar of burnt offering, and poured the rest of it on the ground, then they would receive the remission of a day's worth of sins.

On the other hand, to be forgiven of a year's worth of sins, Leviticus 16:6-10 states, *"Aaron shall offer the bull as a sin offering, which is for himself, and make atonement for himself and for his house. He shall take the two goats and present them before the LORD at the door of the tabernacle of meeting. Then Aaron shall cast lots for the two goats: one lot for the LORD and the other lot for the scapegoat. And Aaron shall bring the goat on which the LORD's lot fell, and offer it as a sin offering. But the goat on which the lot fell to be the scapegoat shall be presented alive before the LORD, to make atonement upon it, and to let it go as the scapegoat into the wilderness."* In the Bible, the scapegoat means "to give out."

In addition, Leviticus 16:29 says, *"This shall be a statute forever for you: In the seventh month, on the tenth day of the month, you shall afflict your souls, and do no work at all, whether a native of your own country or a stranger who dwells among you."*

How were the people of Israel forgiven of a year's worth of their sins all at once? First, they needed the High Priest—in the main passage above, this was Aaron at the time. To make a year's worth of the Israelites' sins, it was absolutely required to have the High Priest. Who, then, was the representative of the priests of the Israelites? It was none other than Aaron. God set aside Aaron and his descendants as the High Priest.

Aaron brought a bull into the Tabernacle's court, passed his sins onto it by first putting his hands on its head to make atonement for himself and his house, cut its throat open, drew its blood, and took some of the blood of the bull and sprinkle it with his finger on the mercy seat on the east side; and before the mercy seat he shall sprinkle some of the blood with his finger seven times. This is how Aaron and his house first received the remission of sin. Atonement means passing one's sins onto the sacrificial animal by putting his hands on its head. The vicarious death of this sacrificial animal is atonement.

The sinful must die because of their own sins, but when they pass their sins onto the sacrificial offering by laying their hands on its head, then this animal is put to death instead. This is how the High Priest and his house were first remitted of their sins. After doing so, he entered into the Tabernacle by himself and offered one of the two goats to God by laying their hands on its head and killing it to take its blood. On behalf of the people of Israel, he then laid his hands on the other goat before their presence and thereby passed their sins onto this goat.

Putting his hands on the head of the goat, the High Priest therefore prayed, "Oh, Lord, the people of Israel have broken Your Law, from the first to the last of Your Ten Commandments, and all the 613 articles of the Law. Lord, all these tribes have become sinners before You. I therefore pass all their sins onto the sacrificial goat by laying my hands on its head." He then cut the goat's throat, drew its blood, and took this blood into the Most Holy, where he was allowed to enter only once a year. He then sprinkled the blood on the mercy seat on the east side, covering the Ark of the Testimony, and before the mercy seat he again sprinkled the blood seven times.

The Ark of Testimony was placed inside the Most Holy. The covering of this Ark was called the mercy seat, and when this covering was removed, one would have seen the two stone tablets of the Ten Commandments, the golden pot that had the manna, and Aaron's rod that budded inside the Ark. Aaron's rod that budded refers to resurrection, the two stone tablets of the Law refers to the righteousness of God, and the golden pot that had the manna refers to God's Word of life. On top of the Ark of the Testimony, a covering called the mercy seat was placed. The blood of the sacrifice was sprinkled seven times before the covering. As bells of gold were attached to the hems of the robe worn by the High Priest, whenever he sprinkled the blood dipped in hyssop, the bells made sound.

As Leviticus 16:14 explains, *"He shall take some of the blood of the bull and sprinkle it with his finger on the mercy seat on the east side; and before the mercy seat he shall sprinkle some of the blood with his finger seven times."* Every time the High Priest sprinkled the blood, the bells rang, and outside the Tabernacle, all the Israelites heard the sound of these ringing bells, for all the sins of the people of Israel could be blotted out only when the High Priest offered this sin offering on their behalf. As such, for the people of Israel, this sound of the ringing bells coming from inside the Most Holy was the blessed sound of the gospel that told them that their sins were all blotted out.

When they heard the golden bells sounding seven times, they told themselves, "I am free now. I had been burdened by all the sins that I accumulated over the past year, but now this burden has been lifted." On this Day of Atonement, the people of Israel won their freedom from all sins, and then went back to their everyday life in joy. Now, in the present, this sound of bells is none other than the very sound of blessings that enables us to be born again of water and the Spirit. The gospel has the power of dynamite that can blow away all sins once and for all.

We have been saved by hearing with our ears, believing in our hearts, and confessing with our mouths our faith in the Word of God, the gospel of the water and the Spirit. The gospel of the remission of sin enables us to be born again of water and the Spirit. Leviticus 16:21-22 states, *"Aaron shall lay both his hands on the head of the live goat, confess over it all the iniquities of the children of Israel, and all their transgressions, concerning all their sins, putting them on the head of the goat, and shall send it away into the wilderness by the hand of a suitable man. The goat shall bear on itself all their iniquities to an uninhabited land; and he shall release the goat in the wilderness."* The offering that thus accepted all the sins of the Israelites passed onto it by the laying on of hands then carried these sins on itself, roaming the sand desert until its ultimate death. This was the Old Testament's remission of sin.

It is written in Jeremiah 17:1 that everyone's sins are written in two places before God. One is God's Book of Judgment, and the other is people's own hearts. As such, to be forgiven by God for our sins, we must receive the remission of our sins, and sins should be erased both in God's Book of Judgment and in our own consciences. Also, we must receive this remission of sin by believing righteously before God.

This is why the High Priest performed the ritual of the sin offering that atoned for all the sins of the people of Israel by putting his hands on the head of the goat in their presence—to show them, in other words, that all their sins were indeed passed onto the goat.

When people hear this good news of the gospel, some people realize it soon, while others are slow to understand it. Those who say, as soon as they hear, "If I had been sinful but my sins were passed onto the goat, then it is the goat that now has these sins"—these are the ones whose realization is quick. When our sins are passed onto the sacrificial offering, then we become sinless. How simple is this? Once one realizes it, truth is easy to grasp. When the goat disappears from the sight and the man who sent it off returns, the goat then roams in the wilderness with neither vegetation nor water, and in the end dies with the sins of all the Israelites on its shoulder.

This is how the righteous law of God, that "the wages of sin is death," was fulfilled. God, in other words, saved the nation of Israel by sacrificing this goat, the sacrificial offering, for their sake. God passed all the sins that all the Israelites had accumulated all year long onto the goat, and thereby saved them.

In the New Testament, Jesus has given us salvation by being baptized and crucified (Matthew 3:15-17; 1 Peter 3:21).

Sermon on the Holy Son 3

Why Did Christ Die Vicariously for Many?

It was because Jesus was baptized by John, through which He accepted the sins of the world passed onto Him. In Matthew 3:15, we see Jesus taking all the sins of the world upon Himself by receiving His baptism from John. The reason why Jesus was baptized by John was because He had to shoulder the sins of the world through this baptism. It was because this was God's own desire, as stated in Isaiah 53:10, *"Yet it pleased the LORD to bruise Him...."* Therefore, the purpose of God in sending Christ to this earth was to *"bruise Him"* because of His bearing of our sins and death.

Realizing this love, the Apostle John said, *"In this is love, not that we loved God, but that He loved us and sent His Son to be the propitiation for our sins" (1 John 4:10).* In obeying the will of God, Christ therefore discarded at once the comfortable way, which He was more than capable of taking with His majesty and power, and did not hesitate to eschew the compassion of His disciples and the great welcome of the people. Put differently, because there was a way for Him to accept all the sins of the world by being baptized, He died for us, who, as Isaiah 53:6 tells us, *"like sheep have gone astray,"* and has thereby opened *"a new and living way" (Hebrews 10:20).* Jesus, in other words, had to embrace His baptism by John to satisfy the righteousness of God, regardless of whether people would recognize it or not, for this was the very desire of the Father. This is why He faced the accursed and terrifying death of the Cross.

Because His sufferings were the will of God, He remained completely silent even as He suffered. As Isaiah 53:7 states, *"He was oppressed and He was afflicted, Yet He opened not His mouth; He was led as a lamb to the slaughter, And as a sheep before its shearers is silent, So He opened not His mouth."* As such, even as He was falsely accused, harshly beaten, plucked of his beard, and spat at, because He had accepted the sins of mankind passed onto Him from John through His baptism, He remained silent.

Not only this but furthermore, because it was the will of the Father for Him to be baptized and thus die, He died for the sake of those who believe. Only after being baptized by John at the age of 30 and thereby taking upon Him the sins of the world, our Lord was crucified at the age of 33 and shed His blood. He then rose from the dead, and has become the eternal Savior for those of us who believe in this truth.

Sermon on the Holy Son 4

We Must Firmly Believe in The Resurrection of Jesus

The Apostles affirmed their faith in the resurrection of Jesus by confessing, with the Apostles' Creed, "The third day He rose again from the dead."

Acts 1:3 says, *"To whom He also presented Himself alive after His suffering by many infallible proofs, being seen by them during forty days and speaking of the things pertaining to the kingdom of God."* The phrase, *"after His suffering,"* refers to the complete death of Christ. There are many proofs showing us that Christ died completely, but in particular, John 19:34 states, *"But one of the soldiers pierced His side with a spear, and immediately blood and water came out."*

The fact that Jesus was crucified to death has been recognized by everyone of everywhere. This punishment of crucifixion, a condemnation that the Romans dealt to foreigners, was a cruel punishment sentenced to political insurgents and slaves. Before the rise of the Roman Empire, crucifixion was generally carried out by hanging a convict on a cross by tying his hands and feet to it, and then killing the condemned by piercing his chest with a spear.

But the Roman version of crucifixion was a punishment that nailed, instead of tying, the hands and feet of a convict to a cross and left him hanging on the cross to die a slow death. As such, it is said that it took a considerable time for the condemned to die, usually 3-4 days, but at times even a week. We cannot even begin to imagine how painful it must have been to be punished in such a way, being nailed, drained of blood, suffering from increasingly unbearable thirst, bombarded relentlessly by the sun, and encircled by flying vultures. The condemned were made to suffer until the very last moment of death. Because of the extreme cruelty of this punishment, the Emperor Constantine, it is said, eliminated this particular form of punishment.

What, then, explains the fact that Jesus died in just six hours? As mentioned above, when one of the soldiers pierced His side with a spear, blood and water came out. As this shows, Jesus died so soon because He suffered such a great heartache for sinners that it literally broke and burst. In other words, He died from a ruptured heart.

In three days after His death, Jesus rose again in a perfect body. What is strange is that despite this, some people hesitate to believe in the resurrected Jesus, even as they profess to recognize His death. This can only be seen as a work of the Devil trying to prevent mankind from believing in this truth, as stated in Luke 8:12: *"Those by the wayside are the ones who hear; then the devil comes and takes away the word out of their hearts, lest they should believe and be saved."* To deny the truth of the resurrection of Jesus, the Devil therefore advocates through unbelieving, secularized scholars such false hypotheses as the apparent death hypothesis, the spiritual resurrection hypothesis, the hallucination hypothesis, the manipulation hypothesis, the stolen body hypothesis, and others. But the verity of the resurrection of Jesus has many definitive proofs, including Acts 1:3.

The Fact That Jesus Presented Himself Alive Is the Proof

Acts 1:3 tells us that Jesus presented Himself alive to His disciples by many infallible proofs. No matter what people say, when our Lord Himself declares to be alive, there is then no ground for any dispute.

Jesus had liberated power over life and death. As John 10:17-18 states, *"Therefore My Father loves Me, because I lay down My life that I may take it again. No one takes it from Me, but I lay it down of Myself. I have power to lay it down, and I have power to take it again. This command I have received from My Father."*

In Revelation 1:18, Jesus also says, *"I am He who lives, and was dead, and behold, I am alive forevermore. Amen. And I have the keys of Hades and of Death."* Our Lord has the power to rise from the dead to live again, for He is God the Almighty and a perfect man at the same time.

"The wages of sin," as Romans 6:23 tells us, *"is death."* This is the unchangeable, righteous law of God. As such, Jesus took care of the sins of the world and blotted them all out through His baptism and blood. Because He made all the sins of the world disappear, He rose from the dead again and has become the God of those who believe in Him. This is how the righteous law of God is established.

That His Tomb Was Empty Is the Evidence

Matthew 27:57-66 tells us that a rich man from Arimathea, named Joseph, laid the dead body of Jesus in a tomb hewn out of rock, and that he sealed the tomb by rolling a large stone against its door. The passage also tells us that a guard was placed at the tomb to secure the tomb. But the tomb became empty as the Lord rose from the dead with His power and came out of His tomb. Luke 24:3 says, *"Then they went in and did not find the body of the Lord Jesus."* What else can this be but the proof of the Lord's resurrection?

Jesus is a great, historic figure. One of the proofs is the chronological use of *Anno Domini* (A.D.), which means "in the year of our Lord." Years and months have been set, in other words, based on the day of His coming. He is the Lord of history, creation and salvation. If He had not been able to rise again from the dead, His tomb would have remained closed as a great historical landmark. The tombs of the great figures of history still remain as places of great interest. For example, Confucius' tomb is in China, Buddha's tomb is found in India, and that of Mohammed is at Mecca, Saudi Arabian.

If Christ had not risen from the dead again, His tomb should still remain closed like theirs. But because He rose from the dead in three days, His tomb has been opened. This is believing in our Lord, the one and only God.

That He Ate after He Rose from the Dead Is the Proof

Spirits do not eat. But the resurrected Lord ate. Luke 24:40-43 states, *"When He had said this, He showed them His hands and His feet. But while they still did not believe for joy, and marveled, He said to them, 'Have you any food here?' So they gave Him a piece of a broiled fish and some honeycomb. And He took it and ate in their presence."* Acts 10:40-41 also testifies, *"Him God raised up on the third day, and showed*

Him openly, not to all the people, but to witnesses chosen before by God, even to us who ate and drank with Him after He arose from the dead." That Jesus ate provides us the explicit proof of His resurrection.

In 1 Corinthians 15:3-4, Paul also testifies, *"For I delivered to you first of all that which I also received: that Christ died for our sins according to the Scriptures, and that He was buried, and that He rose again the third day according to the Scriptures."* The Bible is the inspired Word of God with absolute authority that can be neither added to nor subtracted from. As this Bible had prophesied, Jesus died and rose again.

Around the time of Jesus' death, His disciples had been trembling in fear. But after they were convinced of His resurrection, they became bold to spread through Jesus the resurrection from the dead. As Acts 4:18-20 tells us, *"So they called them and commanded them not to speak at all nor teach in the name of Jesus. But Peter and John answered and said to them, 'Whether it is right in the sight of God to listen to you more than to God, you judge. For we cannot but speak the things which we have seen and heard."* Peter and other Apostles also replied, *"We ought to obey God rather than men" (Acts 5:29).*

Although Jesus' disciples had trembled before the dead Jesus, once they saw the living Jesus, they became bold. From then on to the very present, the reason why the saints have spread this gospel even as they have been persecuted for Christ, and why they have been willing to die for its sake, is because of the certainty of the resurrection of Christ and the assurance of their own resurrection as well.

Jesus' resurrection is a prelude to our own resurrection. In 1 Corinthians 15:20, it is stated, *"But now Christ is risen from the dead, and has become the firstfruits of those who have fallen asleep."* As such, the teachings of the Pauline Epistles are also centered around, first of all, the core truth of the resurrection of Jesus Christ, and then on the message that this resurrection also brings us our own resurrection.

Sermon on the Holy Son 5

The Proof That Jesus Ascended to Heaven

The Bible Written by the Inspiration of the Holy Spirit Testifies to This Truth

Acts 1:1-2 testifies the Ascension of Jesus Christ saying, *"The former account I made, O Theophilus, of all that Jesus began both to do and teach, until the day in which He was taken up, after He through the Holy Spirit had given commandments to the apostles whom He had chosen."*

Christianity is not a theory-driven religion, but it is the real truth. The Bible thus is authoritative. In particular, the Gospel according to Luke is not a product of the physician Luke's subjective and superficial knowledge, but it is the living record that "through the Holy Spirit" he wrote of Jesus' ministry "until the day in which He was taken up." When we can believe in historical documents left behind by mere mortals, how can we not believe in this Bible that was written through the inspiration of the Holy Spirit, who is God Himself?

The above passage testifies that Jesus ascended to Heaven before the presence of many who witnessed this with their own eyes. Acts 1:9 says, *"Now when He had spoken these things, while they watched, He was taken up, and a cloud received Him out of their sight."* 1 Corinthians 15:6 also states, *"After that He was seen by over five hundred brethren at once, of whom the greater part remain to the present, but some have fallen asleep."* Since Jesus resurrected while over 500 saints were witnessing it, His ascension is the undeniable reality. And this was written when most of those who witnessed it were still alive.

That Jesus Returned Again to the Infinite from the Finite Realms Testifies to His Ascension

We must believe as a matter of course that the infinite Lord came to this finite world incarnated in the flesh of mortals, took upon our sins by being baptized, was crucified, rose from the dead again with His power, and, as the glory of this resurrection, ascended to Heaven returning to the infinite from the finite.

If we the saints were, after coming to and staying on this earth for a while, to return to Heaven, then there is nothing strange about this but it is only a matter of course. Likewise, there is nothing strange in the fact that Christ, who came from Heaven, stayed on this earth for a while and then ascended back to Heaven again, but it is only a matter of course. Our Lord therefore said to Nicodemus, to whom He had explained the principles of Heaven but who could not understand, as the following: *"Are you the teacher of Israel, and do not know these things? Most assuredly, I say to you, We speak what We know and testify what We have seen, and you do not receive Our witness. If I have told you earthly things and you do not believe, how will you believe if I tell you heavenly things? No one has ascended to heaven but He who came down from heaven, that is, the Son of Man who is in heaven" (John 3:10-13).*

That Jesus Ascended to Heaven before the Witnessing of Many Testifies the Truth

In Acts 1:10, it is said, *"And while they looked steadfastly toward heaven as He went up...."* Here, the phrase, *"looked steadfastly toward heaven,"* means that they looked toward Heaven very closely. In other words, it shows that the Lord's ascension took place before the very eyes of the disciples over an extended time-period. Put differently, this experience of the disciples was not just instantaneous, but it provided clear and detailed evidence. That the disciples *"looked steadfastly"* means that they gazed for a considerable length of time. Jesus' ascension was not a momentary and instant event, like a falling star or lightening in the night sky, but it was a concrete and certain event. Like this, Christianity is the very witnessing of the real truth.

Two Angels Bore Witness

In the latter half of Acts 1:10, it is written, *"two men stood by them in white apparel."* These two men here clearly refer to angels. The "white apparel" symbolizes purity and honor. Both the Old and New Testament testify alike that angels always manifest in the likeness of human beings (Matthew 28:3; Luke 24:4; Acts 10:30; Genesis 18:2, 19:1; and Revelation 21:17).

Angels are supernatural beings who are sinless. As such, their testimony plants the truth in our hearts, as refreshing as the clear water of a river.

Our Lord Who Will Return in the Same Manner as His Ascension

Acts 1:11 says, *"Men of Galilee, why do you stand gazing up into heaven? This same Jesus, who was taken up from you into heaven, will so come in like manner as you saw Him go into heaven."*

After the Lord's ascension, the 500 brothers gathered to bear witness to this ascension were still staring at the empty sky in sadness even as the Lord had disappeared from their sight. To give them comfort, courage and hope, the two angels testified, *"This same Jesus, who was taken up from you into heaven, will so come in like manner as you saw Him go into heaven."*

The phrase *"in like manner"* means that just as He had ascended to Heaven from the Mount of Olives, the returning Lord would invariably come back to this Mount of Olives (Zechariah 14:4), and He promised that at this time, He will not come in humility as He did when He first came, but He will come in clouds in glory. Therefore the righteous can wait for Him in hope, saying, "Come, Lord Jesus!" (Revelation 22:20)

Sermon on the Holy Son 6

The Lord Will Return as The Lord of Judgment

< Revelation 20:11-15 >

"Then I saw a great white throne and Him who sat on it, from whose face the earth and the heaven fled away. And there was found no place for them. And I saw the dead, small and great, standing before God, and books were opened. And another book was opened, which is the Book of Life. And the dead were judged according to their works, by the things which were written in the books. The sea gave up the dead who were in it, and Death and Hades delivered up the dead who were in them. And they were judged, each one according to his works. Then Death and Hades were cast into the lake of fire. This is the second death. And anyone not found written in the Book of Life was cast into the lake of fire."

This world will be judged by the Lord for its sins. In particular, we must pay attention to the fact that the Lord Himself will be the Executor of the Last Judgment. As such, the Apostles' Creed confesses, "(I believe in) He ascended into heaven, and sitteth on the right hand of God the Father Almighty; from thence He shall come to judge the quick and the dead."

In all things, if there is a beginning, then there must be an end. As God Himself, Jesus therefore is both the Creator and the Judge. Because the Lord is the Savior of mankind, He is also the Judge. He is "the first and the last."

The Bible tells us that there is the due season for everything under heaven. As Ecclesiastes 3:1 says, *"To everything there is a season, A time for every purpose under heaven,"* and Acts 17:31 says, *"because He has appointed a day on which He will judge the world in righteousness by the Man whom He has ordained."* As such, God will most certainly judge the sins of mankind. The standard of this judgment is measured by whether or not one had believed in the gospel of the water and the Spirit, and everyone will be judged based on this criterion.

The Time of Judgment

The Day of Judgment will come when God has completely spread the gospel of the water and the Spirit throughout the whole world (Matthew 24:14). This will be the final day of this world, the day of its end. This is the day referred to by Revelation 20:11, which says, *"Then I saw a great white throne and Him who sat on it, from whose face the earth and the heaven fled away. And there was found no place for them."*

It is also stated in 2 Peter 3:10, *"But the day of the Lord will come as a thief in the night, in which the heavens will pass away with a great noise, and the elements will melt with fervent heat; both the earth and the works that are in it will be burned up."* Moreover, not everyone can escape the judgment of God, but it can be avoided only by believing in the gospel of the water and the Spirit given by the Lord. The Scriptures refer to this day as the *"Day of Judgment" (Matthew 11:22, 12:36; Acts 17:31)* and the *"Day of God's Wrath" (Romans 2:5; Revelation 16:1).*

The Purpose of God's Judgment of This World

Psalm 97:2 says, *"Righteousness and justice are the foundation of His throne."* As such, the purpose of God's judgment of this world is to reward the righteous and to punish sinners.

Only the omnipotent and omniscient Lord of righteousness will clearly separate His sheep from the goats (Matthew 25:32), and His wheat from the chaff (Matthew 3:12). As such, when the last day comes, those who believe will be unmistakably distinguished from those who do not.

The first half of Revelation 20:11 says, *"Then I saw a great white throne and He who sat on it."* This tells us that no one can hide his/her sins from Him. As such, people must either receive the remission of all their sins once and for all, by believing in the gospel of the water and the Spirit given by the Lord, or otherwise they must be destroyed. Who can ever pretend to be righteous before the Lord (Psalm 143:2)? Let us, therefore, confess our sins and believe in the gospel of the water and the Spirit. As God has told us in Proverbs 28:13, *"He who covers his sins will not prosper, But whoever confesses and forsakes them will have mercy."*

The Nature of Judgment

The nature of God's judgment of sinners can be understood when we first comprehend the essence and attributes of the Lord, who is this very Judge. This judgment is a judgment rendered within God's mercy, and therefore there is no other mercy. If God were to judge sinners without first having blotted out their sins with the gospel of the water and the Spirit, He would indeed appear to us as a terrifying God. But because Jesus has blotted out all our sins of the world through His baptism and the blood of the Cross, it has been determined by God that those who believe would be saved and those who do not would be judged.

This is why Hebrews 9:27 says, *"And as it is appointed for men to die once, but after this the judgment."* In Matthew 25:31-33, Jesus Himself said, *"When the Son of Man comes in His glory, and all the holy angels with Him, then He will sit on the throne of His glory. All the nations will be gathered before Him, and He will separate them one from another, as a shepherd divides his sheep from the goats. And He will set the sheep on His right hand, but the goats on the left."* He also said in verse 46, *"And these will go away into everlasting punishment, but the righteous into eternal life."*

Because we are finite mortals, even as we believe, in our lack of understanding and impetuous disposition we wish that all the problems of this world would be resolved. But Jesus will judge those who do not believe in the remission of sin that He has given them.

Revelation 20:12 states, *"And I saw the dead, small and great, standing before God, and books were opened. And another book was opened, which is the Book of Life. And the dead were judged according to their works, by the things which were written in the books."*

There are two kinds of books before God, and they are the Book of Life and the books of deeds, that is, the Books of Judgment. These are the benchmark of judgment. The books in the above passage refer to the books in which all the deeds of mankind are recorded. The Law points out sins, and it teaches us that whoever does not believe in the gospel of the water and the Spirit given by the Lord will not be able to be saved from all sins. That God would thus judge mankind with His books of deeds and the Book of Life is the righteous judgment. Depending on whether we believe in Jesus Christ as God, and whether we believe in the gospel Word of the water and the Spirit that He has given us, our names are written in the book of deeds or in the Book of Life. And based on this record, we will be either rewarded or punished.

When Thomas Edison, the king of invention, heard his own voice played back from the phonograph that he had invented, He said, "Even man can hear his own recorded voices. Would God, then, not have recorded all our deeds also? "

Although such world-renowned celebrities as Gary Cooper, Marilyn Monroe, John Wayne, and Bruce Lee have passed away this world long ago, their voices, expressions, and acts are still seen through TV sets, just as lively now as in their past. When mere mortals can achieve this with their limited knowledge and technology, wouldn't the Almighty God be able to accomplish this?

As such, the question of faith—that is, whether one believes in the baptism of Jesus and the blood of the Cross—is more important than even the question of his/her life and death. Why? Because depending on whether this person believes in the gospel of the water and the Spirit or not, he/she will either receive the remission of sin from God, or face the condemnation of sin from Him.

The Law of God enables us to recognize our sins. And going before the presence of Jesus Christ, His baptism and blood lead us to believe in the remission of our sins. When measured by God's Law, no mankind can ever be said to be sinless. But once people believe in the gospel of the water and the Spirit, they can then no longer be said to be sinful. This is so because the Law of God not only sees outward acts of sin, but it pierces into the deepest recess of the human heart. The Law says, for example, *"Whoever looks at a woman to lust for her has already committed adultery with her in his heart."* Likewise, even if we had not actually killed anyone, if we had hatred, jealousy, or envy that forms our murderous motivation, the Law tells us that we have already killed (Matthew 5:21-22, 27-28).

Moreover, even if we had kept God's Law well, when we break it even once, then we are deemed to have broken all of it. This is why mankind must believe in the gospel of the water and the Spirit given by the Lord.

God has therefore given to mankind Jesus Christ, who has completed the righteousness of God for all of us apart from the Law (Romans 3:21). Whoever believes that this Christ, obeying the Law completely, was baptized, shouldered the sins of the world, and died on the Cross can be saved from all his/her sins, just by believing in this truth. This is the covenant of salvation received by faith (Romans 5:19).

By accusing our hearts with the sins of the world, the Devil tries to drag us to hell. But by the advocacy of Christ, those of us who believe are forgiven of our sins and therefore enter Heaven. This is why 1 John 2:1 states, *"If anyone sins, we have an Advocate with the Father, Jesus Christ the righteous."*

In this light, the eternal judgment between Heaven and hell is not decided by our good or evil deeds, but it is decided by whether or not we believe in the baptism and blood of Jesus Christ, and whether or not we believe Him to be God. As such, that everyone should, while in this world, believe in the gospel of the water and the Spirit given by Christ is the most important truth.

Our Lord Himself said, *"And as Moses lifted up the serpent in the wilderness, even so must the Son of Man be lifted up, that whoever believes in Him should not perish but have eternal life. For God so loved the world that He gave His only begotten Son, that whoever believes in Him should not perish but have everlasting life" (John 3:14-16).*

Jesus, who was baptized by John to take upon the sins of mankind and to fulfill all righteousness, carried these sins of the world to the Cross. Those in this world who believe in Jesus Christ are saved from all their sins. Because Jesus was baptized to vicariously bear the sins of mankind and died on the Cross, even a murderous robber like Barabbas was also saved. As such, mankind can avoid judgment only by returning to Christ as soon as possible and believing in Him.

While living, all human beings are standing at a crossroad, where they must choose between the two ways to the opposite destinations—eternal destruction and eternal life.

Sermon on the Holy Son 7

Who Will Be Subjected to Judgment?

As Apostles' Creed states, "(I believe in) from thence He shall come to judge the quick and the dead," the entire mankind, from its father Adam to the end of the world, will be subjected to God's judgment. Hebrews 9:27 says, *"And as it is appointed for men to die once, but after this the judgment."* As such, if it is true that all who are born as human beings must die, then it cannot be anything but true that the judgment would follow after this.

At the beginning of Revelation 20:12, it is stated, *"And I saw the dead, small and great, standing before God."* Here, the phrase "small and great" does not mean adults and children, but the "great" refers to kings, presidents, and other such high-ranked politicians and the powerful, while the "small" refers to ordinary citizens and common people.

Also, at the beginning of Revelation 20:13, it says, *"The sea gave up the dead who were in it."* This means that all those who died of accidents will also stand before the throne of judgment. No matter where people might die, whether in the sea, the air, or the land, because the whole heaven and earth are in God's hands, no one can avoid His judgment.

In the middle of the above verse 13, it says, *"Death and Hades delivered up the dead who were in them,"* and continuing on with verse 14, it says, *"Then Death and Hades were cast into the lake of fire. This is the second death."*

Sin is the unchanging law that puts people to death, and Hades is the prison that confined the dead. But now, when the judgment comes, even these will be changed and release the dead in obedience to the law of resurrection. In other words, when eternal life and destruction are determined by the Last Judgment, there will no longer be the rule of death and Hades. This is why these two things are cast into the lake of fire.

Put differently, that Death and Hades are cast into the lake of fire means that the sinners standing before the throne of judgment will be cast into the lake of fire. This is when death, the last enemy of life, will be destroyed (1 Corinthians 15:26), and it means that the Beast and the false prophets will first be cast into the lake of fire (Revelation 19:20), followed by Satan, the head of demons, who will also be cast into hell (Revelation 20:10).

Tertullian, a Church Father, warned of the impending judgment of the Romans who fed the believers to hungry lions in public arenas and coliseums, or crucified and burnt them, and who watched and enjoyed such spectacles, by saying to them, "You love spectacles. Wait in anticipation, for you will see the Last Judgment, the greatest spectacle of all."

Indeed, there will be no greater spectacle than this, for every mankind who ever lived on this earth, high or low, and from the ancient to the middle and into the present times, will face the Last Judgment and either enter Heaven of eternal life or cast into the destruction of soul.

Revelation 20:15 is the conclusion. It says, *"And anyone not found written in the Book of Life was cast into the lake of fire."* Whoever wants to have his/her name written in the Book of Life must be born again of the water and the Spirit spoken of by the Lord. To be born again of water and the Spirit, we must pass all our sins onto Jesus through His baptism, and we must die on the Cross with the Lord. Only then can we be born again of water and the Spirit and receive eternal life.

Sermon on the Holy Son 8

What Is the Faith That God Declares to Be Great?

< Matthew 8:5-10 >

"Now when Jesus had entered Capernaum, a centurion came to Him, pleading with Him, saying, 'Lord, my servant is lying at home paralyzed, dreadfully tormented.' And Jesus said to him, 'I will come and heal him.' The centurion answered and said, 'Lord, I am not worthy that You should come under my roof. But only speak a word, and my servant will be healed. For I also am a man under authority, having soldiers under me. And I say to this one, 'Go,' and he goes; and to another, 'Come,' and he comes; and to my servant, 'Do this,' and he does it.' When Jesus heard it, He marveled, and said to those who followed, 'Assuredly, I say to you, I have not found such great faith, not even in Israel!'"

The Faith of the Centurion

Now when Jesus had entered Capernaum, a centurion came to Him, pleading with Him, saying, "Lord, my servant is lying at home paralyzed, dreadfully tormented." And Jesus said to him, "I will come and heal him." The centurion answered and said, "Lord, I am not worthy that You should come under my roof. But only speak a word, and my servant will be healed. For I also am a man under authority, having soldiers under me. And I say to this one, 'Go,' and he goes; and to another, 'Come,' and he comes; and to my servant, 'Do this,' and he does it." When Jesus heard it, He marveled, and said to those who followed, *"Assuredly, I say to you, I have not found such great faith, not even in Israel!"*

There are people in this world who, like this centurion, have the faith that believes everything is fulfilled only by the Word of Jesus. We can see that it is those who have such faith who are blessed, and that this centurion of such faith has the same faith of the born-again. The centurion, feeling compassion for one of his subordinates who was paralyzed, came to Jesus seeking to heal him. We can see that this centurion shared his fate and went through thick and thin with the men under his command, and that he had a great love for them.

The centurion earnestly begged Jesus for the healing of his servant, and Jesus permitted it. From the passage, we can clearly find out that the disposition of this centurion's faith was such that he believed Jesus to be the Son of God. He believed in Jesus' Word of truth—that is, he believed that Jesus was the Son of God who would raise the dead and heal us wholly from our sins.

"Lord, I am not worthy that You should come under my roof. But only speak a word, and my servant will be healed." The centurion said this not because he did not want Jesus to come to his house, but because he had faith in the Word of God first. If people are disposed to serve and revere God, then through the Word of God, such people can receive the remission of their sins, have faith planted in them by the Word, and also receive blessings from this written Word of God. This

faith is the faith of the centurion.

Even if we have nothing in our hands, if we only believe in the Word of God, the abundant blessings of God can be all ours. From the passage above, we can find out just how great the centurion's faith was.

What is the wholesome faith? Believing in God who has fulfilled and will fulfill everything only by His Word is the wholesome faith. When you have the knowledge of the Word of God and faith in this Word, you will then also receive wonderful blessings in your lives, just like the centurion.

The centurion asked Jesus to only speak a word; such faith is a great faith. Those who revere and fear God believe that His great power can, just by the Word of God, save us from our sins, enabled us to receive eternal life, and make us live our lives in blessings. God's blessing can come about only by believing in His Word. The faith that believes in the Word actually enables us to live a new life.

John 8:32 states, *"And you shall know the truth, and the truth shall make you free."* When we dwell on the Word of God and believe in the Scriptures as they are, this Word then works in our hearts in concrete ways, transforms our surroundings, our souls, and ourselves, and thereby enables us to enter Heaven instead of hell.

It is wrong to attend church even as one does not have faith in the Word of God. If one does not believe in the Word of God, then attending church is only a mere religious practice, something that one does on his/her own and has nothing to do with salvation.

This centurion's faith is the faith that believes in God and in His Word. Long ago, there used to be many who believed in the Word. Our fathers of faith such as Abraham, Isaac, and Jacob had the faith in His Word. Abraham followed the Word

(Genesis 12:4), and Isaac, following his father's path, also believed in the Word of God that Abraham had believed. Abraham believed in God's Word that He would give him his descendants and land as it was, and passed it onto his son Isaac. And God, in fact, did allow Abraham's descendants to have the land of Canaan, today's Israel.

By believing in the Word, we became the born-again righteous and God's children. What is truly marvelous is how they became righteous in the first place. Did they become righteous by receiving God through their ardent prayers, speaking in tongues, healing miracles, or holy praises? Can we receive God just by confessing Him as our Father?

True Faith Is to Believe the Word of God

Faith in God cannot come about by emotions, devotion, or one's own abilities. I have seen many Christians giving their ardent prayers of repentance in tears, confessing their sins out loud. Generally speaking, it has become a customary practice for Christians who have attended church for a long time to try to wash away their sins through their prayers of repentance given with many tears. Our era has been turned into a corrupted one, where Christians, seeing such outward displays, approve each other's faith based on this.

Heresies are interested in the charismatic movement, mysticism, and materialism. And they are prone to pursue such erroneous tendencies tumultuously and desperately. But all their followers, while they may get transient comfort and satisfaction out of such beliefs, cannot but continue to live confused lives with empty hearts. This can be the evidence that such people have not been born again, nor received the Holy

Spirit, further less believed in the Word of God. Believing in Jesus is to believe in the Word of God.

Jesus said that the faith of the centurion was great. Let's find out why He said so. Sinners who can neither believe nor follow the Word of God cannot understand the righteous who have the faith in God's Word.

In particular, the charismatic movement, into which sinners are prone to fall, claim that speaking in tongues is the evidence that proves one's receiving of the Holy Spirit, of becoming God's child, and of salvation itself. They therefore speak in tongues everywhere. But most Christians who claim to speak in tongues actually speak in false tongues. The born-again cannot stand to be near those who speak in tongue. Satan works so deceptively in the charismatic movement that those who believe in supernatural visions and powers, and those who seek after signs, miracles, and visions apart from faith in the Word of God, cannot even come close to the faith of the centurion. Their faith is a pseudo faith that is fundamentally different from the faith of the centurion, and that seeks only after what cannot be seen by the eye.

The centurion's faith was one that believed in everything that Jesus Christ said, confessing, *"But only speak a word, and my servant will be healed."* Believing that whatever God says will all be fulfilled accordingly, in other words, is this faith of the centurion.

For today's Christians, speaking in tongues does not mean that they have received the remission of sin, nor that they have become God's children. Neither does seeing visions mean that they have been born again, nor does claiming to have spiritual gifts mean that they have the born-again faith.

Strictly speaking, it is because such people have no faith that they hold onto mystical things. These things are given by

Satan. Such mystical faith can last only a week at most. After only a few days, they begin to search for the Lord again, looking for where they can find miracles and signs. This is the proof of the fact that they have no Holy Spirit in their hearts.

If Jesus, the Word of God, is in us, and if we have received the remission of sin and the Holy Spirit indeed dwells within us, then we will never fall into such traps. Nor can we ever work with them, for we are fundamentally incompatible with them, and, above all, our very seed is different from theirs. The faith of the centurion is the same as ours.

The grace of God that He has bestowed on us is so great that He has allowed us, unlike those who pursue signs and miracles, to believe and follow His Word. I can therefore only thank Him.

Having faith and becoming the righteous come about only by believing in the Word of God. When sinners deny their own thoughts, reveal their true selves before the Word of God, humbly listen to what the Word tells them, and truly believe in it, they can then become righteous. This is the power of God and the power of His Word. They can thereby enter the Kingdom of Heaven, and become God's own children.

We can live blessed lives in gratification and joy. But all these blessings come about by the Word of God, for this is the truth itself. Seeing the centurion's faith, our Lord said, *"Your faith is great."* Someone who is paralyzed cannot do anything on his/her own. Likewise, sinners cannot make their sins disappear on their own. But they can be wholly forgiven of their sins only by the Word of God, and this is the faith that our Lord spoke of by referring to the faith of the centurion.

We have received the remission of sin by believing in the Word of God. Then after, we acknowledged that how important for us to have faith in His Word. Before we are born again, we cannot realize how essential it is to have the faith in the Word. Only the Word of God can blot out our sins. It is because the centurion had this faith that he said, *"But only speak a word, and my servant will be healed."*

Our sins cannot be blotted out by our own efforts, nor by anything else but the Word of God. They can be blotted out only by the Word of God. It is by believing only in God's Word of the truth of the water and the Spirit that we are saved, not by the man-made thoughts, doctrines, efforts, repentance, and sanctification of our own making. Salvation received in dreams or visions is no salvation. The remission of sin received not from God's Word of being born again of water and the Spirit is not salvation.

There are many who become even greater sinners even as they profess to believe in Jesus and attend church. Hebrews 1:3 says, *"upholding all things by the word of His power, when He had by Himself purged our sins."* The reason why such people become even more sinful and are not freed from their sins despite believing in Jesus is because they do not know the Word of God correctly. He who has cleansed away all the sins of mankind is Jesus. Because what Jesus has done is written in detail in the Word of God, it is by believing in this Word that we can become righteous and live our lives in such blessings.

Those who have not received the remission of sin from the Word, whoever they might be, are all liars. Jesus is the way and the life. No matter how people kneel down and how ardently they give their prayers of repentance during the worship service, leaving the Word of God aside, this cannot enable them to enter Heaven. The efforts, devotions, and works of human beings cannot blot out their sins. The kind of faith and the remission of sin that is not constituted by the Word alone all belongs to the devil.

Nothing in this world, even if it were the power to drive out demons, can enable people to be loved by the Lord, and even if they were martyred, this does not mean that their souls are saved. If people do not constitute their faith concretely on the Word, it will inevitably change in the end. All the components of their faith, such as their faith in God, in salvation, and in His judgment, will change as times go by. All such things are completely futile.

People who claim to have traditions, who pride in their lineage and pedigree, and who boast of their denominations, of their faith, and of what they have done—these people assure themselves to be God's people. But God said that He would cast out such people to hell. It would be even okay to take pride if they believe in the Word as it is. However, because they do not do so but believe in Him based on their own standard, God said that He would cast them out to darkness.

Matthew 7:23 states, *"I never knew you; depart from Me, you who practice lawlessness!"* What is lawlessness? Lawlessness refers to the deeds of those who claim to believe in God and exercise His power even as they do not actually have faith.

God's Church is where we listen to the Word of God. It is a place where we can set aside our own thoughts, and instead hear and follow the Word. There are people who claim that even as they remain sinful, they can enter the Kingdom of God because they attend church and believe in Jesus. Those who speak of orthodoxy are even more zealous, saying that they are "the saved sinners." Even as their hearts have no faith, they profess to believe in God and claim that He will take them to Heaven. See for yourself if you can find anywhere in the Bible where such claims are backed in writing.

The saints refer to those who are sinless—that is, they

refer to the righteous. People who boast of orthodoxy say, "God has admitted us as righteous even as we are sinners, but this does not mean that we are actually sinless." But God does not justify us because we attend church. Far from it, people who claim that they can enter the Kingdom of God by the works of their faith are only loving God in an unrequited love, for their salvation is of their own making, not received from the Lord by faith. Such people cannot be saved. The sins in their hearts are the evidence of their not having been saved. Whoever has sin carved in their hearts, even if he/she believes in the Lord, will be cast into hell.

Having blotted out all the sins of the world, Jesus has told us to believe in Him. God is pleased by those who believe in Jesus, are freed from their sins, and have become the righteous. God has prepared Heaven for the righteous. "Lord, I believe that You took away all my sins. But please wash away this sin that I have. Please forgive me for this sin." If anyone prays in this way, then this can only mean he/she does not truly believe in God's gospel, and is only turning God into a liar.

Those who condemn themselves even as they believe in Jesus are nothing more than heretics. We must realize correctly that there is no more condemnation in Jesus Christ (Romans 8:1). The sinful cannot blot out the sins of other sinful souls with the Word, but they only end up turning them into sinners who believe in Jesus somehow, just like themselves. But those who have received the remission of their sins can, because of this powerful Word of the remission of sin in them, lead the sinful to also become sinless. This is how we become righteous by believing in Jesus.

Blessings are to be born again by the Word of God. Blessings are to follow the spiritual leader, and to unite together in serving the church and spreading the gospel of the remission of sin to souls. The centurion, even though he was a Gentile, believed in the Word of God as it was. He thus was saved, and became a perfect and righteous person. In contrast, those who boasted of themselves as orthodox Jews were abandoned, for they did not know Jesus correctly. Which is right?

Faith in the Word enables us to move from a life of sin to a life of salvation, and it allows us to be blessed by all the Word. Faith in God is believing in Him and His Word. It was because the centurion had the faith that God declared to be great. Such faith is in us by the grace of God, for we believe that His Word has been and will be fulfilled exactly as it is.

For people who still do not have this faith of the centurion, if they would just believe in the Word of God, by this faith they will all become like the centurion. The faith that is most approved by God is the one that believes in what God has said as it is. Believing in God who has made us sinless is the faith of the centurion.

Sermon on the Holy Son 9

What Is the Gift That Moses Commanded as a Testimony?

<Matthew 8:1-4>

"When He had come down from the mountain, great multitudes followed Him. And behold, a leper came and worshiped Him, saying, 'Lord, if You are willing, You can make me clean.' Then Jesus put out His hand and touched him, saying, 'I am willing; be cleansed.' Immediately his leprosy was cleansed. And Jesus said to him, 'See that you tell no one; but go your way, show yourself to the priest, and offer the gift that Moses commanded, as a testimony to them.'"

Sin Is Compared to Leprosy

Jesus tells us here that those who have received the remission of sin should give the gift that Moses commanded as their testimony. They say that it takes six years from the time of leprosy infection for people to realize its subjective symptom. The disease remains dormant for the first 6 years, but on the 7th year it breaks out openly. This is a particular pathological characteristic of leprosy.

The main passage above tells us about Jesus healing a leper from his disease. This is a true story that actually had happened, and through the story, God also reveals the nature of our sins, as well as telling us that He has solved the problem of these sins once and for all.

The leper in the above passage earnestly wanted to be healed from his disease, and this is why he came before Jesus Christ as it was, without hiding but revealing his disease. This leper believed that nothing could not be achieved by the Word of Jesus, and he also believed that it was more than possible for Jesus' Word to heal his own disease.

Seeing this leper's faith in the same eye as that of the centurion of the same chapter, Jesus cleansed him. The core lesson of this account is not about the actual healing of the disease per se, but it is about how we can be healed from the disease of our sins.

The leper here alludes to the fact that we have in our hearts the malady of sin, like leprosy. From the very moment of our birth from the womb of our mothers, we were all born with the disease of sin. When we were first born, we could not realize that we were such evil sinners, but once we grew up to a certain age, we came to realize that we were in fact evil, that others were also evil, and that all human beings are evil.

But God tells us, through the passage above, that if these completely evil human beings come to Jesus and reveal their true selves without hiding, and if they have the faith that says, "If You are willing, I believe that You are more than able to cleanse even such a sinful being as I," Jesus will then indeed gladly heal them from their sins.

Did the Lord heal the leper at once or twice? The passage tells us that Jesus healed the leper at once. Our sins are healed not in several stages, but all at once. If we have faith in the

Word of God, then by coming to know and believe in the God who has blotted out all the sins of mankind once and for all, we can receive the remission of sin all at once. Our sins are never healed in several stages.

A woman who had been suffering from hemorrhage was healed once and for all just by touching Jesus' garment (Mark 5:29). She was freed from not only the symptom of bleeding, but its very cause. Naaman, commander of the army of the king of Syria, was also healed from leprosy all at once (2 Kings 5:14), and the leper in the passage above was immediately cleansed from his leprosy as well.

What Is the Difference between the Religious and the People of Faith?

Because of their foolishness resulting from their ignorance of the truth, the religious believe that they can receive the remission of sin through their daily repentance, even as they live everyday in sin. But for the people of faith who follow the Word, all the problems of their sins have been solved once and for all, and they live in the midst of the grace of God.

Church means the gathering of those who follow Jesus Christ. We must realize that the Sadducees and the Pharisees, even as they professed to believe in God, were not the ones who were healed by Jesus, but those who were healed by Him all at once were only those who, like the hemorrhaging woman and the leper, could not do anything about their illnesses on their own.

If it were possible for us to solve the problem of sins in our hearts by our own works, prayers of repentance, and good deeds, there would have indeed been no need for Jesus to come to this earth. And if we believe that we can solve the problem of sin in this way, we will never be able to meet Jesus for the rest of our lives. But the problem of our sins cannot be solved no matter what we do and how hard we try, and we are such beings who cannot but sin regardless of how we try not to.

Because our sins do not disappear no matter how much we repent, we must realize clearly that the problem of sin just cannot be solved by our own strengths and confess before God that we are sinners. We must also realize the truth that when we thus confess, "I am a sinner before God"—neither out of humility nor out of doctrinal conviction but of our sincere hearts—and when we come before God's presence and ask for His mercy, He will solve away all our problems of sin once and for all, just as He had healed the leper.

Only those who reveal themselves before God as complete sinners, ask for His mercy, and confess to Him, "I cannot avoid but be cast into hell, for I am sinful. Lord, please have mercy on me." Only such people can receive the grace of the Lord.

Romans 3:10 declares, *"There is none righteous, no, not one."* This verse is what the Apostle Paul spoke to those who had not yet received the remission of sin. Did Jesus not come to this world to make sinners righteous? There is no such thing as half-made remission of sin, nor is there any half-righteous. However, unfortunately, there are so many such weird people in today's Christianity. They believe that sins are forgiven whenever they give prayers of repentance. Our sins are not something that can be blotted out by our prayers of repentance.

Jesus is the One who perfectly completed the healing of sin. Jesus does not speak of our sins by dividing them into original sin and personal sins, nor does He say that while He took away our original sin, our daily sins must be forgiven by offering the prayers of repentance. The faith of those who believe so is a half-faith, and such people will live the rest of life as sinners, die as sinners, and be cast into hell as sinners.

God does not accept half-faith. If you believe, then you must believe 100 percent, and if you do not believe in any slightest bit of the truth, then you do not believe 100 percent—there is no such thing as believing 50 percent. Jesus does not call us sinless by thinly covering our sins even as we remain sinful because of our disbelief. When we know the Bible correctly, we can find out that Jesus calls us sinless because He actually removed our sins beforehand and completely blotted them out.

Among the religious leaders of Christianity at the present, there are those who claim that Jesus took away our original sin but not our personal sins. The Bible does not speak of the original and personal sins, and no mention of such things is found in it. Before Jesus, all sins, great and small, from those we were born with to those that belong to us and those that we commit with our own acts—indeed, every possible sin—are the same, all manifested as the sins of the world. Water is water, whether it is sewage water or tap water.

No one knows for sure when people started to distinguish their original sin from their personal sins. Because many Christian leaders themselves have not been born again, they do not know how to solve all the problems of sin, and because they do not know, they have turned Christianity into a mere religion, claiming that God would forgive our sins if we 'repent' our sins. The word 'repent' is far different from the word 'confess' (1 John 1:9).

What is repentance? It only means to turn around; it does not mean praying for God to forgive us of our sins. God has said that He wants us to give Him offerings that ask for His mercy and grace. Having compassion for the souls heading to hell because of sin, God wants to save us—this is what His heart is all about. What His heart desires is to make the sinful beings sinless and holy through Jesus Christ and thereby enable them to take part in His Kingdom, and He has indeed fulfilled this completely.

Romans 6:23 states, *"For the wages of sin is death, but the gift of God is eternal life in Christ Jesus our Lord."* The sinful has no other way but to be cast into hell, but the gift of God is to live with the Lord forever. God's gift for us is making us sinless.

There are too many people in these days who, by believing in the remission of sin in too humanistic and man-made ways of thinking, are headed straight to hell. They think that they can enter Heaven by their own acts of devotion, such as faithfully giving tithes, coughing up a lot of offerings, giving prayers of repentance, and attending every morning prayer service. But all these are flawed.

Let's assume that someone just died and went before God. Standing before His presence, this person says, "This sinner of many iniquities has come before You, Lord." What would our Lord say? He will say what He said in Matthew 7:21-23: *"Not everyone who says to Me, 'Lord, Lord,' shall enter the kingdom of heaven, but he who does the will of My Father in heaven. Many will say to Me in that day, 'Lord, Lord, have we not prophesied in Your name, cast out demons in Your name, and done many wonders in Your name?' And then I will declare to them, 'I never knew you; depart from Me, you who practice lawlessness!'"*

God is not the Father of sinners, nor the Lord of the sinful, but the Father of the righteous and the Lord of the born-again who have received the remission of sin. Even if the above person were to say, "Lord, how come you do not know me? For

You, I did my utmost to testify Your name, and I had dedicated my whole life to You," God will simply reply, "How do you pretend to be My child when you are sinful. Be cast into hell, you who practice lawlessness!"

The first priority for sinners is to receive the remission of their sins by believing in the Word right now. This is what is most urgently required. How can we gather sinners who have not even received the remission of sin in our churches and then call them as saints? Where on this earth can anyone find sinful saints? The sinful are not the saints, but they are simply sinners.

God declares in Hosea 4:6, *"My people are destroyed for lack of knowledge. Because you have rejected knowledge, I also will reject you from being priest for Me; Because you have forgotten the law of your God, I also will forget your children."*

Knowing God is the foundation of knowledge, and yet human beings can neither read His mind nor put down their own knowledge built like the Babel Tower, but they devote even more efforts to their own acts and deeds. This is why God says, "I do not know you."

We can be made sinless only by believing purely in the Word, 100 percent of it. We must have the faith that completely entrusts everything to God, saying, "You can make me clean." The faith of the so-called incremental sanctification, which claims that God cleanses us gradually in steps, is not the faith of true salvation.

Christ's faith is not constituted by a mere religious practice through which we can reach our salvation by our own efforts and moral training like Buddhism's emphasis on goodness and mercy, but it is constituted by the salvation of grace coming down from above without our own efforts—that is, by the one-sided love of the Lord that has delivered the drowning people from their certain death.

Just as the leper was instantaneously healed by the love and power of our Lord, we, too, can also be saved from the sins of our hearts by this love and power of the Lord. When our Lord healed the leper, He said to him, *"See that you tell no one; but go your way, show yourself to the priest, and offer the gift that Moses commanded, as a testimony to them."*

The Gift That Moses Commanded Refers to the Lamb of God

Leviticus 1:1-4 says: *"Now the LORD called to Moses, and spoke to him from the tabernacle of meeting, saying, 'Speak to the children of Israel, and say to them: 'When any one of you brings an offering to the LORD, you shall bring your offering of the livestock—of the herd and of the flock. 'If his offering is a burnt sacrifice of the herd, let him offer a male without blemish; he shall offer it of his own free will at the door of the tabernacle of meeting before the LORD. Then he shall put his hand on the head of the burnt offering, and it will be accepted on his behalf to make atonement for him.'"*

We can see from verse 2 that *"the gift that Moses commanded"* is a livestock, either of the herd or the flock. After giving His Law to mankind, God showed them the Tabernacle in order to enable them to realize that they were sinners. Through the sacrificial system of this Tabernacle, He has taught us how He would pass all the sins of the Israelites—and our own sins also—onto the sacrificial lamb and thereby forgive us.

God loved us, and to save us from our sins, He prepared the sacrificial offering that had to die vicariously in our place. This is the sacrificial lamb and bull. When priests put their hands on the head of the burnt offering, the offering was accepted by God, and this offering then atoned us.

When people are receiving the laying on of hands from someone who is demonically possessed, then they also become the demon possessed. The laying on of hands means "to pass on"; when the High Priest laid his hands on the head of a goat, the sins of Israel were then passed onto its head (Leviticus 16:21). When the sins were thus passed onto the goat, and when this goat was killed in our place and its blood was offered to God, God then accepted this blood and forgave their sins.

How have we received the remission of our sins? We must bear witness to this. The evidence of salvation must be sought after only with the Word, and it is not proven by the evidence of seeing visions, prophesizing, or speaking in tongues. It is only with the Word of God that we can prove how we had been sinners and how we have now been saved from all our sins. This proof bears witness before God, before Satan, and before human beings.

Leviticus 4:27-31 states, *"If anyone of the common people sins unintentionally by doing something against any of the commandments of the LORD in anything which ought not to be done, and is guilty, or if his sin which he has committed comes to his knowledge, then he shall bring as his offering a kid of the goats, a female without blemish, for his sin which he has committed. And he shall lay his hand on the head of the sin offering, and kill the sin offering at the place of the burnt offering. Then the priest shall take some of its blood with his finger, put it on the horns of the altar of burnt offering, and pour all the remaining blood at the base of the altar. He shall remove all its fat, as fat is removed from the sacrifice of the peace offering; and the priest shall burn it on the altar for a sweet aroma to the LORD. So the priest shall make atonement for him, and it shall be forgiven him."*

When the common people or priests sinned unintentionally, they brought a lamb, passed their sins onto it by laying their hands on its head, and then offered it to God. The laying on of hands means the passing of sin, and sacrifice means dying vicariously in someone else's place.

Through the daily offerings, God is showing us that Jesus came to this earth, and just like these lambs and goats, He accepted all the daily sins passed onto Him by John the Baptist.

All the people of Israel in the Old Testament received the remission of their sins by believing in this. When they sinned unintentionally, recognizing their sins through the Law, they immediately brought a lamb and confessed their sins by putting their hands on its head. The priests then accepted this offering, cut its throat open, drew its blood, put the blood on the horns of the altar of burnt offering, and then sprinkled the rest on the ground and the altar. This is how the Israelites received their remission of sin.

The horns of the altar of burnt offering refer to the Books of Deeds, that is, the Books of Judgment. Whenever we sin, God writes our sins into the Books of Judgment in His Kingdom, and He also writes them into our hearts. Because human beings are so shameless and try to deceive even God, He records their sins in the Books of Deeds and their own hearts. This is why when those who have not received the remission of sin pray, the sins in their hearts come out, and they come to pray, "Lord, please forgive this sinner." Therefore we must know how Jesus, coming to this world, accepted all our daily sins passed onto Him. Only then can we be freed from our sins.

When the people of Israel sinned, they brought a lamb, passed their sins onto its head by laying their hands on its head, and were thereby forgiven of their sins. The priests then killed this lamb and put its blood on the horns of the altar of burnt offering. Blood is the life of all flesh (Leviticus 17:14). Blood atones sin. When this blood was put on the four horns, God, seeing this, knew that their sins were already judged through the lamb, and thereby did not condemn those who had passed their sins onto the lamb.

That God therefore put to death animals instead of people was the very love of God. When people sin, they must surely die, but because God loved them, He had animals killed in their place. This was the daily offering established by God of justice.

Leviticus 16:29-34 states, *"'This shall be a statute forever for you: In the seventh month, on the tenth day of the month, you shall afflict your souls, and do no work at all, whether a native of your own country or a stranger who dwells among you. For on that day the priest shall make atonement for you, to cleanse you, that you may be clean from all your sins before the LORD. It is a sabbath of solemn rest for you, and you shall afflict your souls. It is a statute forever. And the priest, who is anointed and consecrated to minister as priest in his father's place, shall make atonement, and put on the linen clothes, the holy garments; then he shall make atonement for the Holy Sanctuary, and he shall make atonement for the tabernacle of meeting and for the altar, and he shall make atonement for the priests and for all the people of the assembly. This shall be an everlasting statute for you, to make atonement for the children of Israel, for all their sins, once a year.' And he did as the LORD commanded Moses."*

The above passage describes the ritual of the Day of Atonement, which God made the Israelites to give to Him through the High Priest once a year for those who could not give offerings everyday and for the entire people of Israel. Through this offering, the entire people of Israel received the blessing of having a year's worth of their sins all remitted.

Leviticus 16:6-10 states, *"Aaron shall offer the bull as a sin offering, which is for himself, and make atonement for himself and for his house. He shall take the two goats and present them before the LORD at the door of the tabernacle of meeting. Then Aaron shall cast lots for the two goats: one lot for the LORD and the other lot for the scapegoat. And Aaron shall bring the goat on which the LORD's lot fell, and offer it as a sin offering. But the goat on which the lot fell to be the scapegoat shall be presented alive before the LORD, to make atonement upon it, and to let it go as the scapegoat into the wilderness."*

God gave the Israelites the sacrificial system through which they could pass on not only daily but also a year's worth of their sins onto the offering and be forgiven of these sins once and for all. Aaron was Moses' older brother and the High Priest. Aaron took one of the two goats into the court of the Tabernacle and passed the sins of all the people of Israel onto it by laying his hands on its head. He then killed the goat and took its blood inside the veil, into the Most Holy. This blood was absolutely required to enter inside the veil of the Most Holy.

The Tabernacle was divided into the Holy Place and the Most Holy. The High Priest could enter into the Most Holy where the Ark of the Testimony was placed only by carrying the blood of the sacrifice. It was by seeing this blood that God allowed Aaron to enter into the Most Holy. Having killed the goat that had accepted the sins of all the people of Israel, Aaron then went into the Most Holy with this blood and sprinkled with his finger on the mercy seat on the east side seven times.

Because bells were attached to the robe of ephod, whenever he sprinkled the blood, they made sound, and with this sound of bells heard by the people of Israel gathered outside the Tabernacle, God confirmed to them that their sins were indeed atoned before Him.

Leviticus 16:20-22 states, *"And when he has made an end of atoning for the Holy Place, the tabernacle of meeting, and the altar, he shall bring the live goat. Aaron shall lay both his hands on the head of the live goat, confess over it all the iniquities of the children of Israel, and all their transgressions, concerning all their sins, putting them on the head of the goat, and shall send it away into the wilderness by the hand of a suitable man. The goat shall bear on itself all their iniquities to an uninhabited land; and he shall release the goat in the wilderness."*

Of the two goats, the remaining one was the scapegoat, *"aza'zel"* in Hebrew (meaning "she-goat to let go"). Before all the people of Israel watching outside the gate of the Tabernacle, Aaron confessed all the iniquities of the Israelites, put all these sins on the head of the goat by laying his hands on its head, and sent it out to the vast, empty wilderness to die. The sacrificial offering that shouldered sins was to die surely. By sacrificing this goat, God freed all the people of Israel from their sins. None other than this is the offering that Moses commanded. All the people of the Old Testament received the remission of their sins in this way.

Through this sacrificial system, God foretold us that Jesus would come to this earth, shoulder the sins of mankind just like this goat, and blot out all their sins, committed daily and through out their entire lifetime. The people of the Old Testament received the remission of sin through this sacrificial offering. Now, you, the people of the New Testament, must realize just how God has solved the problem of all the sins of the world and of all your sins, and how He has given you the remission of all these sins.

The Old and New Testaments match with each other. We should now find out from the New Testaments what Jesus has done for us.

Sermon on the Holy Son 10

The Baptism of Jesus and The Remission of Sins

< Luke 1:5-17 >

"There was in the days of Herod, the king of Judea, a certain priest named Zacharias, of the division of Abijah. His wife was of the daughters of Aaron, and her name was Elizabeth. And they were both righteous before God, walking in all the commandments and ordinances of the Lord blameless. But they had no child, because Elizabeth was barren, and they were both well advanced in years. So it was, that while he was serving as priest before God in the order of his division, according to the custom of the priesthood, his lot fell to burn incense when he went into the temple of the Lord. And the whole multitude of the people was praying outside at the hour of incense. Then an angel of the Lord appeared to him, standing on the right side of the altar of incense. And when Zacharias saw him, he was troubled, and fear fell upon him. But the angel said to him, 'Do not be afraid, Zacharias, for your prayer is heard; and your wife Elizabeth will bear you a son, and you shall call his name John. And you will have joy and gladness, and many will rejoice at his birth. For he will be great in the sight of the Lord, and shall drink neither wine nor strong drink. He will also be filled with the Holy Spirit, even from his mother's womb. And he will turn many of the

children of Israel to the Lord their God. He will also go before Him in the spirit and power of Elijah, 'to turn the hearts of the fathers to the children,' and the disobedient to the wisdom of the just, to make ready a people prepared for the Lord.'"

Who Is John the Baptist?

God sent His Son Jesus as the One who *"will save His people from their sins" (Matthew 1:21).* To take upon the sins of mankind, the Creator of the universe Himself incarnated through the Virgin Mary and came to this earth as the Lamb of Sacrifice. Jesus' ministries began with His baptism. When Jesus turned 30, He was baptized by John the Baptist.

Who is John the Baptist? Jesus Himself testified that John is the representative of all mankind. Matthew 11:11-13 states, *"Assuredly, I say to you, among those born of women there has not risen one greater than John the Baptist; but he who is least in the kingdom of heaven is greater than he. And from the days of John the Baptist until now the kingdom of heaven suffers violence, and the violent take it by force. For all the prophets and the law prophesied until John."* Jesus said that among those born of women there has not risen one greater than John the Baptist. The one, who was greater than all the prophets of this earth such as Isaiah, Ezekiel, and Habakkuk, and greater than even Moses of the Old Testament, was none other than John the Baptist, the representative of all mankind.

In the Old Testament, the chosen ones of the male descendants of Aaron were anointed as the High Priests. Like the High Priests who passed the sins of the people of Israel onto the goats by laying their hands on its head as the representative of the Israelites, to blot out all the sins of mankind God had to raise John the Baptist as the representative of all mankind and have him pass the sins of the world. God sent John the Baptist to this earth as the last prophet. And the last High Priest was none other than John the Baptist.

As God made sure to pass the sins of all the people of this world only through the descendants of Aaron, He chose a descendant of Aaron as promised—that is, John the Baptist, the greatest of all those born of women—and sent him to this world six months earlier than Jesus to turn many people to *"the wisdom of the just, to make ready a people prepared for the Lord" (Luke 1:17).*

In this way, God raised John the Baptist as the representative of mankind, and through him God passed our sins onto Jesus. John the Baptist came before Jesus as a witness, and from the Word we must find out how he bore witness.

As Aaron passed the sins of the people of Israel to the goat on the Day of Atonement, John the Baptist baptized Jesus Christ and thereby passed all the sins of mankind onto Him. It testifies to us how all our sins have been blotted out.

The Mystery of Jesus' Baptism

As mentioned before, Jesus was baptized by John the Baptist, as described in Matthew 3:13-17. Because people generally are baptized without even knowing its meaning, baptism is handed out too carelessly to whoever has memorized the Ten Commandments, promises to keep the Lord's Day, and is willing to recognize the Lord Jesus as his/her Savior. Those who are baptized with a clear understanding of the true meaning of this baptism are extremely rare.

Coming to this earth, Jesus was baptized by John the Baptist, and we must realize why He had to be baptized. We must question why Jesus, who was sinless, had to be baptized. But those who have not received the remission of sin are neither curious about the baptism of Jesus nor are able to know it at all. The mystery of this baptism can be known by only those who have received the remission of sin.

Jesus is the High Priest of the Kingdom of Heaven. And John the Baptist is the representative and High Priest of all mankind. John the Baptist had the authority to pass all the sins of mankind, and Jesus, the Heavenly High Priest, accepted all these sins passed onto Him by giving up His own body as the sacrificial offering before God, and has thereby blotted out the sins of all human beings.

Matthew 3:15 states, *"Permit it to be so now, for thus it is fitting for us to fulfill all righteousness."* Jesus was baptized at the Jordan River, the river of death. Baptism means to pass on, to be submerged, to cleanse, to burry, or to transfer, and it has the same meaning as the Old Testament's laying on of hands. As sins were passed onto the sacrificial offering when hands were laid on its head, all our sins were passed onto Jesus when John the Baptist baptized Him. In other words, it was because all the sins of mankind were passed onto Jesus that He was buried vicariously as the sacrificial offering in our place and was condemned. The ritual by which Jesus thus accepted all the sins of mankind from John is baptism.

That Jesus came to this world and was baptized was to fulfill all the righteousness of mankind and to forgive the sins of every human being with no exception. Was Jesus baptized because He was humble? That was never the case. Jesus spoke to John, *"permit it to be so now."* Because Jesus came to this world to take upon the sins of mankind, He said, "You shall pass sins to Me and I shall accept them, for it is My task to become the scapegoat before your sight and thereby forgive all your sins."

Because of our sins, we are bound to hell, tormented, and deceived by Satan, but Jesus came to save such people as us, to make us righteous and turn us into God's children.

When Jesus was baptized and came out of water, the Holy Spirit descended like a dove and testified that He was the Son of God. The Holy Spirit is the One who bore witness, meaning that God Himself testified that His Son Jesus accepted all the sins of mankind through His baptism.

Because the sins of mankind were actually passed onto Jesus, God tells us that we are sinless. Had Jesus not taken away all sins when He came to this earth, we would still remain as sinners no matter how ardently we believe in Him. Having blotted out all sins, God is telling us, *"Believe on the Lord Jesus Christ, and you will be saved, you and your household" (Acts 16:31).* It is by believing that we receive eternal life.

John 1:29 says, *"The next day John saw Jesus coming toward him, and said, 'Behold! The Lamb of God who takes away the sin of the world!'"* John the Baptist continued to shout out to people that all the sins of mankind were passed onto Jesus through His baptism. It is none other than John the Baptist who shouted, "He is the Son of God, the Lamb of God who takes away the sin of the world."

What Is the Sin of the World?

Jesus took away the sins of the world. Jesus took them

away by being baptized. Having thus borne the sins of mankind with His baptism, Jesus had to give up His life on the Cross. Jesus took all the sins of the world upon Himself. Through His baptism, He took away the sins of our own fathers and mothers also, for they, too, are the people of the world. All the sins that we commit throughout our entire lifetime, including the sins that we commit without realizing, are the sins of the world. These sins were also passed onto Jesus through John the Baptist. The sins that we committed in our teenage years are also the sins of the world, and so these sins were also passed onto Jesus. Jesus did not just take away the sins of a few special people, but He took away all the sins of every human being.

But only those who believe in this truth, that Jesus accepted our sins through John the Baptist and has forgiven them all, are saved. If we do not believe in this, we cannot but be cast into hell because of it. The gate of Heaven has already been opened a long time ago, but if our hearts still do not believe in the truth, we cannot be saved.

People go to hell because they do not believe in the truth of the water and the Spirit, and because they do not know it. Jesus took away all our sins of the world. All the sins that we have committed, whether in our childhood, in our teens, or in our adulthood, are "the sins of the world," and they were therefore all passed onto Jesus. Jesus is the Son of God who took upon each and every one of our sins, without ever dividing them into the original and personal sins.

Are the sins that we commit in midlife and senior years not the sins of the world? These are also the sins that we commit in this world, and so Jesus took upon these sins as well. Because His love is eternal and vast, Jesus did not divide our sins into the original and personal sins but accepted them all through His baptism.

Had Jesus died on the Cross without first being baptized when He came to this earth, then His death would have been in vain. That we have believed in the Lord and labored for His sake would also be in vain. Were the sins of our own children passed onto Jesus? Let us check.

If you still remain single but will get married and have kids, your children's sins are also the sins of the world, and therefore they, too, were all passed onto Jesus. The sins of your grandchildren and of their descendants were also passed onto Jesus, and Jesus has atoned for all these sins as well. The weaknesses of mankind are also the sins of the world. However Jesus took upon these sins through baptism and shed His blood on the Cross.

Jesus said in John 8:32, *"And you shall know the truth, and the truth shall make you free."* And it is true. People who keep the Sabbath only as a matter of denominational doctrines and believe that although Jesus took away the original sin they still have to repent their daily sins cannot but continue to become even more sinful. Although they try to live according to the Word of God and do good deeds, the more they try, the more difficult it becomes to devote themselves. They can realize themselves that they are becoming even more sinful before God.

In Jesus Christ, we have already died with Him for our sins, and we have also become alive with Him. There is no other thing that you and I now have to do but to be saved by believing in Jesus, the Savior of sinners who took upon Himself all our sins with His baptism, carried the sins of the world to the Cross and died on it. Believing in this truth, the gospel of the water and the Spirit, is the way to receive eternal life. ⌧

PART

III

Sin

III. CONFESSION OF FAITH IN THE HOLY SPIRIT

"I believe in the Holy Ghost,
the holy catholic Church, the communion of saints;
the forgiveness of sins;
the resurrection of the body;
and the life everlasting. Amen."

The Triune God

Must Christians know God the Father, the Son, and the Holy Spirit as one God, and confess their faith in all of them? Yes. The reason is as follows.

God the Father, the Son, and the Holy Spirit all led the ministry of creation and gave life to mankind. But God the Father is the Father of the Holy Son. The Son fulfilled the ministries of the remission of sin—that is, He was baptized by John and crucified to save mankind from sin. The Holy Spirit took the task of bearing witness to those who believe that the baptism of Jesus and the blood of the Cross fulfilled the works of the atonement of mankind.

For us to become the perfect people of God, we need the

faith that believes in God the Father, the Son, and the Holy Spirit in this way. It is because God the Father, the Son, and the Holy Spirit created the universe and us that we have come to exist in this world, and for God the Son to save sinners from their sins, the baptism that fulfilled the righteousness of God and the work of bloodshed on the Cross was required. Because Jesus was baptized by John and thereby took upon the sins of the world, He bore the punishment of these sins that we were supposed to bear and died on the Cross vicariously in our stead.

By doing so, those who believe could finally be freed from all their sins. This truth had been prepared long before, and it is the core ministry of the gospel of the water and the Spirit. It is only when we apply this truth to us that Jesus Christ's work of atonement finally become a work fulfilled for our own sake, and we can be saved from all our sins by believing.

If we had no knowledge of God the Father, the Son, and the Holy Spirit, then we would have been unable to know how the universe was created and who has given us life, and if there had not been God the Son, neither would we have been able to know the way of salvation—that is, how we could pass on our sins—nor what is the basis of our salvation from sin. But if there had been no Holy Spirit bearing witness, then no matter how great of a way of salvation has been prepared, this truth would have been just a pie in the sky, having nothing to do with us at all. Therefore, whenever we confess the faith of the Apostles' Creed, we must think of God the Father, the Son, and the Holy Spirit who has created us and given us life, and we must stand firmly on our faith in the truth that these three independent Persons are one God for us.

God the Holy Spirit

God the Holy Spirit Is Not Just A Power, But He Also Has Character

The Holy Spirit, *"Ruwach Qadowsh"* in Hebrew, and *"pneuma hagios"* (πνεύμα ἁγίος) in Greek, is the third Person of the Trinity.

The Apostles' Creed makes a very terse confession of faith in the Holy Spirit, only stating, "I believe in the Holy Spirit." It is very important that the saints know correctly who the Holy Spirit is and what His works are. And we must also know about the gifts of the Holy Spirit, which will be discussed later part of this section.

When we confess that we believe in the Holy Spirit, before we think of some mystical power possessed by Him, we must first pay particular attention to the fact that we receive the Holy Spirit only when we believe in God the Father and the works of the Son. Many Christians have a tendency to think that they can receive the Holy Spirit whenever and as frequently as they need Him, but this is a profoundly mistaken thinking. We must realize that the Holy Spirit is not an angel, but He is God to whom we must given our worship and praise. As such, we can receive the Holy Spirit when we believe in God the Father and the works of the Son.

What God the Holy Spirit Does

What, then, does God the Holy Spirit do? First, the Holy Spirit participates in the ministries led by God the Father and the Son. The Holy Spirit participated in the works of creation and providence unfolded by God the Father. Not only this, He also participated in the works of salvation accomplished by God the Son by bearing witness. This refers to the ministry that the atonement fulfilled by Jesus would be applied and completed to each and every saint.

How Can We Receive the Baptism of the Holy Spirit?

To understand what the baptism of the Holy Spirit is, we need to first understand why Jesus was baptized by John and died on the Cross. As Romans 3:23 states, *"all have sinned and fall short of the glory of God,"* every human being is born as a sinner who cannot but commit iniquities before God, and according to Romans 6:23, which tells us that *"the wages of sin is death,"* each and every one of mankind therefore cannot avoid but be punished to death as the wages of sin.

But God the Father, who loves mankind, has prepared a

way by which we can be cleansed of our sins, judged for and saved from them, all through Jesus. God the Father sent His only begotten Son, Jesus, and poured the punishment, which we had to receive ourselves, on Jesus instead through His baptism and crucifixion. In our place, Jesus took upon our sins and was punished to death by God the Father. However, Jesus, who is unblemished, pure and righteous, then overcame death and triumphed over it. He rose, in other words, from the dead again.

How, then, are these works of atonement fulfilled by Jesus connected to mankind? By believing His works means for us to receive the remission of all our sins. Jesus, who bore all the sins of mankind by being baptized by John at the Jordan River, received all the punishment that He suffered on the Cross to give us the remission of our sins. When we believe that Jesus was baptized by John and suffered His death as the vicarious bearing of our own punishment of sin, the righteousness of God is fulfilled in our hearts.

Furthermore, the righteousness of Jesus is passed onto us as our own righteousness and we are clothed in it, and we therefore come to be considered as the perfectly righteous ones before God, become His children, and partake in eternal life. Galatians 3:27 states, *"For as many of you as were baptized into Christ have put on Christ."*

John 3:16 states, *"For God so loved the world that He gave His only begotten Son, that whoever believes in Him should not perish but have everlasting life."* Like this verse, we become righteous the very moment when we believe that all our sins were passed onto Jesus with His baptism received from John, and believe in the punishment of the Cross.

The word baptism carries several meanings, one of which is to cleanse away sins, and another is to unite. As such, we must realize that "to be baptized by the Holy Spirit" is to know and believe with what method Jesus the Son has solved the problem of the iniquities of sinners, and that it is by this faith that we receive the baptism of the Holy Spirit.

That the Holy Spirit has come into our hearts, dwells in us and unites with us, means that we have believed in the baptism of Jesus. This ministry of the Holy Spirit is well described in the passage from Matthew 3:13-17. Jesus said that the reason why He was baptized by John was to fulfill all the righteous of God with the method of this baptism that He received from John. Therefore, to receive the Holy Spirit, we must first believe that Jesus took upon all the sins of mankind by being baptized by John. This is how we can unite with the Holy Spirit, and the Bible also tells us that we receive the Holy Spirit by believing in the grace of the remission of sin, that Jesus was crucified and shed His blood because He had accepted all the sins of mankind passed onto Him with His baptism. The Holy Spirit dwells in the hearts of those who have been cleansed of their sins with the baptism of Jesus and the blood of the Cross.

This is shown in the conversation that Jesus had with Nicodemus. To Nicodemus who came to see Him, Jesus said that only those who are born again could see the Kingdom of God. Being born again means that a soul that had died because of sin is regenerated as new, and partakes in the eternal life of the Kingdom of God. Hearing about the truth of being born again, Nicodemus was unable to understand what it meant, and so he asked Jesus how such a thing could be happen.

At this time, Jesus answered, *"Most assuredly, I say to you, unless one is born of water and the Spirit, he cannot enter the kingdom of God" (John 3:5).* Only by believing the ministry of Jesus that eliminates all our sins and even the root of our sins, can we be born again as new, and such a wonderful work was fulfilled when He was baptized and died on the Cross. When we believe it, the Holy Spirit dwells within us. No effort, work, achievement, ability, or character of mankind whatsoever is involved in this. We need the faith that believes in the truth that only the baptism of Jesus and His death on the Cross have thus cleansed away the sins of mankind.

We need to pay attention to what Jesus continued to say in His conversation with Nicodemus. Jesus emphasized the importance of the Word that we must be born again of water and the Spirit.

The Holy Spirit's ministry of regeneration that makes our souls born again—that is, the baptism of the Holy Spirit—is not only a transformation that occurs in the profound depth of a person's heart, but it is also an extremely mysterious ministry. Because of this, the ministry itself cannot be seen through our own reason or consciousness. What we can know is that receiving the baptism of the Holy Spirit comes together with the remission of sin that we received into our hearts when we believed in the baptism of Jesus and the blood of the Cross. We realize that we have become God's children when we receive the Holy Spirit as a gift (Romans 8:15).

Who Is the Holy Spirit?

The Holy Spirit refers to the third Person among God. The faith of this Trinity is the most fundamental and core faith. This truth can be all known and understood by believing in the gospel of the water and the Spirit. Why? The reasons are as follows.

1) Because sinners are creatures while God is the far-reaching One who created the vast universe and the entire mankind. As such, the truth of Trinity cannot be known until one receives remission of all sins by believing in the gospel of the water and the Spirit.

2) Because of their transgressions, the hearts of human beings have been darkened by their sins. Just as nothing can be seen when a mirror is stained, the eyes of the hearts of sinners cannot see what the Triune God has done.

3) Without the enlightenment of the Holy Spirit, we cannot know the profundities of God's heart. The Holy Spirit bears witness that the Word of God is the truth (John 16:13). As such, the Holy Spirit enables us to know what the truth of the water and the Spirit is, for He is God Himself who has a complete character in possession of knowledge, emotion and will. He dwells in those who believe in the written Word of God and works with them. We must therefore worship Him, trust in Him, love Him, and obey Him.

What Are the Main Works of the Holy Spirit?

The Holy Spirit does the work of sealing the hearts of the saints who have been forgiven of their sins by believing in the gospel Word of the water and the Spirit.

The Holy Spirit works in our hearts according to our faith in the written Word of truth.

1) He bears witness to the fact that the Word of God is

true. The Holy Spirit guarantees the hearts of those who believe in the Word of the baptism of Jesus and the Cross. As such, when one believes in Jesus' baptism and the blood of the Cross, the One who approves his/her faith as right is God the Holy Spirit. The Holy Spirit works among those who most certainly believe in the written Word. The Holy Spirit approves the faith of those who believe in the gospel of the water and the Spirit. He guarantees, in other words, those who believe that Jesus came to this earth and blotted out the sins of the world with His baptism and blood.

2) The Holy Spirit is with the righteous, and makes them testify the gospel of the water and the Spirit to sinners. In John 16:8-9, Jesus said, *"And when He has come, He will convict the world of sin, and of righteousness, and of judgment: of sin, because they do not believe in Me."* The Holy Spirit reaffirms the gospel of the water and the Spirit in the hearts of the righteous (John 14:26). He bears witness of what the Lord has done. He enable us to know that Jesus came to this earth, took upon the sins of the world by being baptized, and died on the Cross, and He allows us to believe in them.

3) He makes us believe in God and to call upon Him. The Holy Spirits makes the righteous pray. Romans 8:15 states, *"For you did not receive the spirit of bondage again to fear, but you received the Spirit of adoption by whom we cry out, 'Abba, Father.'"* The Holy Spirit enables the saints to call and believe in God as "Abba, Father."

4) The Holy Spirit makes us work with the gifts that He has given us. He enables us to do the works of the righteousness of God with His abilities. 1 Corinthians 15:10 states, *"But by the grace of God I am what I am, and His grace toward me was not in vain; but I labored more abundantly than they all, yet not I, but the grace of God which was with me."*

5) The Holy Spirit leads us until we enter Heaven. The Holy Spirit enables the righteous to keep their faith until they reach the Kingdom of the Lord, and remains with them as their Teacher.

<u>Sermon on the Holy Spirit 1</u>

How Can We Receive the Holy Spirit?

< John 7:37-39 >

"On the last day, that great day of the feast, Jesus stood and cried out, saying, 'If anyone thirsts, let him come to Me and drink. He who believes in Me, as the Scripture has said, out of his heart will flow rivers of living water.' But this He spoke concerning the Spirit, whom those believing in Him would receive; for the Holy Spirit was not yet given, because Jesus was not yet glorified."

Is the Receiving of the Holy Spirit a Separate Experience to a Christian?

Most Christians think that believing in Jesus and receiving the Holy Spirit are two different things. This is why they are trying very hard to receive the Holy Spirit. When most of the believers in Jesus are mired in such confusion, how much frustration would God the Father have! The only way for them to escape from so much confusion is to clearly know the gospel of the water and the Spirit and believe in it.

Jesus said in John 7:38, *"He who believes in Me, out of his heart will flow rivers of living water."* The phrase *"as the Scripture has said"* means that whoever believes in the gospel of the water and the Spirit can receive the Holy Spirit. The Holy Spirit dwells in the hearts of those who believe that Jesus Christ came to this earth by the water and the Spirit and has saved sinners from their iniquities.

When one knows and believes in the gospel of the water and the Spirit, the Holy Spirit then flows in his/her hearts like a river. Jesus said that anyone who thirsts should come to Him and drink. Those in whose hearts the Holy Spirit flows like a river are the ones who have received truly amazing blessings by believing in the gospel of the water and the Spirit. Like this, the Holy Spirit does not come as a separate experience to those who believe in Jesus *"as the Scripture has said."*

Those who earnestly seek to receive the Holy Spirit believe that if they were only to pray ardently and blindly, He would then come down upon them. But such faith has nothing to do with the true gospel that enables us to receive the Holy Spirit given by Jesus.

Thinking that one can receive the Holy Spirit given by the Lord even as he/she rejects or ignores the gospel of the water and the Spirit is not the truth. Without believing in the gospel of the water and the Spirit given by Jesus, we cannot receive the Spirit of God. We cannot buy Him as we buy goods with money. The Holy Spirit comes on us as a gift only when we believe in the gospel of the water and the Spirit.

Why are people unable to have the indwelling of the Holy Spirit in their hearts even as they believe in Jesus? The answer to this question is found in the gospel of the water and the Spirit given by the Lord.

The reason why Christianity has become so murky is because many have misunderstood the Holy Spirit who, as described in Acts 2, came on the Apostles on the Day of Pentecost. Most of them think that the Apostles received the fullness of the Holy Spirit by earnest prayers.

Even though Jesus does not give the Holy Spirit to those who are sinful, there are still many people who persist in their stubbornness. When those who do not know the gospel of the water and the Spirit thirst after this Holy Spirit and insist on their own obstinacy, demons claiming to be Jesus then come into them, and they end up becoming fanatics possessed by these evil spirits. As such, people must not try to receive the Holy Spirit by force in their own stubbornness.

It is very dangerous for someone who has not received the remission of sin to ask for the Holy Spirit. We must realize that this is akin to asking for what is only impossible.

·The Bible says that the authority of those who have received the remission of sin is great. In John 20:23, Jesus said, *"If you forgive the sins of any, they are forgiven them; if you retain the sins of any, they are retained."* As such authority is given to those who have received the Holy Spirit. Their authority is great, and their responsibility is also great. Jesus told Peter, "I give you the keys to Heaven." This is the authority of none of than those who have received the remission of sin through the gospel of the water and the Spirit.

The authority of those who have received the remission of sin and the Holy Spirit into their hearts by believing in the gospel of the water and the Spirit is truly amazing. They have the authority to lead people to the way to Heaven as well to let them to be cast into hell. As such, if the saints do not spread the gospel of the remission of sin to sinners and leave them as they are, then they become the ones who leave these sinners to their destruction. The authority to forgive people's sins is thus given to the saints.

We give our thanks to God for guiding us into the gospel of the water and the Spirit that has enabled us to receive the

Holy Spirit. We have received the Holy Spirit by believing in the baptism of Jesus and the blood of the Cross as the remission of our sins. The gospel of the water and the Spirit is the only true gospel that enables people to receive the Holy Spirit.

Sermon on the Holy Spirit 2

“Did You Receive the Holy Spirit When You Believed?”

< Acts 19:1-7 >

“And it happened, while Apollos was at Corinth, that Paul, having passed through the upper regions, came to Ephesus. And finding some disciples he said to them, ‘Did you receive the Holy Spirit when you believed?’ So they said to him, ‘We have not so much as heard whether there is a Holy Spirit.’ And he said to them, ‘Into what then were you baptized?’ So they said, ‘Into John's baptism.’ Then Paul said, ‘John indeed baptized with a baptism of repentance, saying to the people that they should believe on Him who would come after him, that is, on Christ Jesus.’ When they heard this, they were baptized in the name of the Lord Jesus. And when Paul had laid hands on them, the Holy Spirit came upon them, and they spoke with tongues and prophesied. Now the men were about twelve in all.”

“Did you receive the Holy Spirit when you believed?” Even for Christians, this question is very unfamiliar. The Apostle Paul asked the above believers in Jesus whether they received the Holy Spirit when they first believed, and then testified to them how they, who had believed in Jesus without receiving the Holy Spirit, could receive the Spirit. In the above passage, by once again bearing witness to the power of the baptism of Jesus, Paul renewed their faith.

While Apollos was at Corinth, Paul, having passed through the upper region of the Asia Minor, came to Ephesus, and finding some disciples, he said to them, “Did you receive the Holy Spirit when you believed?” The congregation of the Ephesian Church had been completely ignorant of the truth that they receive the Holy Spirit when they believe in Jesus. Paul then asked them, “Into what then were you baptized?” They answered that they were baptized into John’s baptism.

Paul, in other words, asked the congregation, “Did you receive the Holy Spirit when you believed in Jesus?” This is the difference between Paul and ordinary Christians, and it is also the very difference between those who know the mystery of the baptism of Jesus and those who do not. On the Holy Spirit that one receives when he/she believes in Jesus, the believers at the Church of Ephesus said, *“We have not so much as heard whether there is a Holy Spirit.”* By this, they meant, “How could we have received the Holy Spirit when we haven’t even heard about Him at all?” To them, who did not know the mystery of the baptism that Jesus received, the truth of receiving the Holy Spirit was completely new.

They Should Have Known And Believed in the Baptism That Jesus Received

Hearing that they were only baptized into John’s baptism alone, Paul then explained the relationship between the baptism of Jesus and the Holy Spirit. They therefore believed again in the meaning of the baptism that Jesus Christ received. Like this, there is a huge difference between believing in Him while knowing the meaning of the baptism that Jesus received from John and just believing in Him without this knowledge.

What, then, is the baptism that John gave to people? John told people to repent. This means that he told them to turn away from their sins and return to God. The baptism that John gave was only a baptism of repentance that made people repent. But the baptism that Jesus received from John in Matthew 3:13-17 was received to fulfill all the righteousness of God, and therefore this was different from John's baptism of repentance. The baptism that Jesus received from John was the baptism to take upon all the sins of mankind. As such, their faith was different from the faith of Paul, for the baptism that they received was of not knowing the whole picture of the truth.

What, then, does the baptism that fulfilled all the righteousness of God mean? It means that by being baptized, Jesus took upon all the sins of mankind, from the sins of Adam to the sins of the very last people of the end of humanity.

Matthew 3:15-16 says, *"But Jesus answered and said to him, 'Permit it to be so now, for thus it is fitting for us to fulfill all righteousness.' Then he allowed Him."*

God's righteousness could be attained in the baptism that Jesus received and within the faith that believes in the blood of the Cross.

Why, then, must we be baptized in the name of Jesus Christ? It is because we believe in our hearts that Jesus took all the sins of the world upon His own body by being baptized by John. Therefore, those whose hearts have been forgiven of all their sins by believing in the baptism of Jesus Christ and the blood of the Cross must receive the water baptism again by faith. Why? Because by the faith in His baptism, all the sins in their hearts are now blotted out perfectly, and thus become sinless. This is why Paul explained Jesus' baptism again to those who had not received the Holy Spirit.

The Gospel of Power, of the Holy Spirit, and of Much Assurance

Jesus did not just say in words, "Just believe in me. I am the Savior. If you believe, all your sins will then disappear." Rather, by being baptized, Jesus actually accepted everyone's sins of the world once and for all, and took them all upon Himself. Jesus actually received the baptism from John, and by doing so He actually accepted the sins of the world passed onto Him, went to the Cross, and bore the punishment of sin. His suffering on the Cross made Him shed all the blood that was in His heart. And He rose from the dead again in three days. With His baptism and blood, He has made all the sins of the world disappear, and He has given the Holy Spirit to those who believe as a gift. Jesus is the Savior who has blotted out the sins of the world, and He has given us the gospel of the water and the Spirit that enables us to receive the remission of sin. The baptism of Jesus Christ and the blood of the Cross, in other words, have enabled those who believe to receive the Holy Spirit.

To save sinners from their sins, Jesus was actually born unto this earth through the body of a woman. When He turned 30, He did in fact take all the sins of mankind upon Himself by being baptized. It is because of this that He could be crucified while carrying all these sins of the world and shed all His blood onto the ground. And by rising from the dead again, Jesus has become the actual Savior for those of us who believe in Him.

Do you believe in this truth? Isn't this truth somewhat different from what you had believed before? There is a clear difference, and this is why you must believe in the water and the Spirit from now on. This small difference is what enables and disables people to receive the remission of sin and the Holy Spirit.

The gospel of the water and the Spirit did not just come in words, but it actual came with power. What more can we say? When Jesus accepted the sins of the world passed onto Him through His baptism, was condemned on the Cross, and rose from the dead, we cannot but believe in this. When the Almighty Jesus blotted out all the sins of the entire world with His baptism once and for all, and when He shed His blood, do we then become righteous only by following the Doctrine of Incremental Sanctification? We do not! The true gospel is the gospel of the water and the Spirit.

Before I met the gospel of the water and the Spirit, that is, when I believed only in the blood of Jesus, so-called the gospel was merely an empty story. However, when I believed in the true gospel of the water and the Spirit, and from then on, the gospel in my heart have given me great conviction and power. Paul also states, *"Our gospel did not come to you in word only, but also in power, and in the Holy Spirit and in much assurance" (1 Thessalonians 1:5).* "Did you receive the Holy Spirit when you believed?" When you believe in the gospel of the water and the Spirit, you will receive the Holy Spirit.

Sermon on the Holy Spirit 3.

The Essential Qualification To Be the Apostles

< Acts 1:4-8 >

"And being assembled together with them, He commanded them not to depart from Jerusalem, but to wait for the Promise of the Father, 'which,' He said, 'you have heard from Me; for John truly baptized with water, but you shall be baptized with the Holy Spirit not many days from now.' Therefore, when they had come together, they asked Him, saying, 'Lord, will You at this time restore the kingdom to Israel?' And He said to them, 'It is not for you to know times or seasons which the Father has put in His own authority. But you shall receive power when the Holy Spirit has come upon you; and you shall be witnesses to Me in Jerusalem, and in all Judea and Samaria, and to the end of the earth.'"

In God's plan of salvation, the ministries of Jesus were absolutely required. The contents of these ministries were the baptism that Jesus received from John, His shouldering of the sins of the world and death on the Cross, and His resurrection. A promise was made between God and us that He would give the Holy Spirit as a gift to those who believe in this truth. The Holy Spirit whom God gives to those who have been forgiven of their sins is a gift that is permitted only to those who believe in the gospel of the water and the Spirit exactly as set by God.

Acts 1:4 says, *"And being assembled together with them, He commanded them not to depart from Jerusalem, but to wait for the Promise of the Father, 'which,' He said, 'you have heard from Me.'"* Jesus commanded the Apostles, "To receive the promised Holy Spirit, do not leave Jerusalem but wait." Jerusalem refers to the Church of God spiritually, where the gospel of the water and the Spirit is found. Therefore, God commanded the saints of the Jerusalem Church to stay in the Church to receive the Holy Spirit.

The Holy Spirit Is the Gift to the Born-Again

The Apostles continued to hear the Lord's promise that He would send the Holy Spirit to them. Acts 1:5 states, *"for John truly baptized with water, but you shall be baptized with the Holy Spirit not many days from now."*

We must realize that the Bible tells us that the faith of those who have received the Holy Spirit is not a result of their own acts or deeds, but it is a result of believing in the gospel of the water and the Spirit (Acts 2:38, 3:19). In other words, whether we can receive the Holy Spirit or not is absolutely depended on God's established promise, and not on our own efforts or any spiritual achievements.

As written in the Four Gospels, the Holy Spirit comes inevitably to those who believe in the gospel of the water and the Spirit.

The Spirit of God "is a gift permitted to those who believe in the remission of sin given by Jesus." We can reaffirm in quite a many phrases in the Bible that the Holy Spirit descends on those who believe in the gospel of the baptism of Jesus and His blood. Those who have received the Holy Spirit in the Bible are the ones who believe in the gospel of the water and the blood as their remission of sin.

But from the main passage above, we can see that the power of this Holy Spirit is not for the flesh, but for world mission. *"You shall be witnesses to Me."* The purpose of the indwelling of the Holy Spirit, in other words, is to make us Jesus' witnesses. And for us to become His witnesses means to become His workers who preach the gospel of the water and the Spirit for the rest of our lives. The saints already belong to the Holy Spirit and they are His servants. The Holy Spirit works with the gospel of the water and the blood. This is the power of the true gospel.

When we take a close look at the account on the first Pentecost in Acts 2, we can find that that the baptism of the Holy Spirit on the disciples was for them to spread the gospel of the water and the Spirit given by Jesus. In the ministries of the Holy Spirit, the purpose of His coming must be found in the spreading of the gospel of the water and the Spirit.

When it comes to the "Day of Pentecost," we generally associate it with chaos, set loose the very moment the Holy Spirit descended. In today's time, we associate it with the kind of gatherings where people are lying on the ground—on the pretext that when they received the Holy Spirit they would be filled by the Spirit, fall flat on their backs, and have fellowship with the Lord for days—levitating and shaking uncontrollably, with their hands as if they were shocked by electricity. But this is not the work of the Holy Spirit. The Holy Spirit does not work like this. He works only with and with in God's Word, especially with the gospel of the water and the Spirit.

Do you believe in the gospel of the water and the Spirit

that enables you to receive the Holy Spirit? Or are you still seeking after man-made methods to receive the Holy Spirit? Does the Holy Spirit come when people repent their sins with their prayers of repentance, or when they abandon their idols? Do we receive the Holy Spirit by praying?

What truly enables us to receive the Holy Spirit is the gospel that came about by the baptism and blood of Jesus. There is no other way but to know the gospel of the baptism and blood of Jesus, the gospel that allows us to receive the Holy Spirit given by God, and to believe in and accept this gospel into our hearts.

The descending of the Holy Spirit on the Day of Pentecost was the fulfillment of the Word of prophecy given through the Prophet Joel (Joel 2:29). And God gives the Holy Spirit to those who, now in this age, believe in the gospel of the water and the Spirit. The Holy Spirit comes to those who believe in the gospel that has forgiven and blotted out all the sins of the entire world through the baptism of Jesus, His blood on the Cross, and His death and resurrection. You, too, will surely receive the Holy Spirit as a gift when you believe in the gospel of the water and the blood.

What Kind of Gospel Did Jesus' Disciples Believe?

The disciples were the ones who believed in the baptism and blood of Jesus that He received and shed to save sinners. Why? The reason is well described in the passage from Acts 1:21-26. When the Apostles selected another Apostle to replace Judas, they selected someone who believed that Jesus' baptism through which He took upon all the sins of mankind. In other words, having faith in Jesus' baptism was the most important qualification for the disciples to be the supplementary Apostle. Of course, they had to believe in the truth that Jesus was the Son of God and had become the Savior of sinners. Here, we can know the faith of the Apostles. In short, the disciples of Jesus believed in His whole public ministries: His baptism, crucifixion, death on the Cross, and resurrection. Like this to become an Apostle, one had to believe in the baptism that Jesus received to take upon the sins of the world.

To become His disciples in this last age, we, too, have to believe in the truth of the water and the Spirit. If people ignore any single element of Jesus public ministries—His being Godhood, His baptism through which He took upon the iniquities of sinners (Matthew 3:15), His bloodshed on the Cross, and His death and resurrection, then they cannot become His disciples. Do you believe in Jesus while ignoring His baptism? Then, you cannot receive the remission of sin, but will be destroyed as a sinner instead. For all of us to become Jesus' disciples, we must believe in the baptism that He received and in the blood of the Cross.

To those who have the same knowledge of truth as the Apostles of God had, He has filled them with the Holy Spirit. Like this, we can also receive the Holy Spirit only when we have the faith that believe in the baptism that Jesus received from John, His death on the Cross, and His resurrection.

Before the advent of the Holy Spirit on the Day of Pentecost, the disciples had been weak and cowardly. But when God poured the Holy Spirit on them as He had promised to the Prophet Joel, they all became strong and bold to preach the gospel of the water and the Spirit publicly.

Sermon on the Holy Spirit 4

When Does the Holy Spirit Come?

< Acts 2:1-4 >

"When the Day of Pentecost had fully come, they were all with one accord in one place. And suddenly there came a sound from heaven, as of a rushing mighty wind, and it filled the whole house where they were sitting. Then there appeared to them divided tongues, as of fire, and one sat upon each of them. And they were all filled with the Holy Spirit and began to speak with other tongues, as the Spirit gave them utterance."

When Did the Holy Spirit Come to This Earth?

Now, I would like to explain how the Holy Spirit comes to people.

The main passage of Acts 2 tells us that the Holy Spirit descended on the disciples on the Day of Pentecost. Does this mean that they, who had already received the Holy Spirit, received more fullness of the Spirit? We must find out about this first.

Some people claim that after believing in Jesus, we must once again receive the Holy Spirit such as the phenomenon shown in Acts 2. We must ponder upon this claim and examine how nonsense such a claim is.

As a matter of fact, those who make such a claim do not know the truth revealed in the Bible. We receive the Holy Spirit as a gift simultaneous to the remission of sin that we receive when we believe in Jesus (Acts 2:38). How can we receive the Holy Spirit separately, only after a considerable lapse from the time when we first believed in Jesus? Such faith is not the correct faith. Even now, there are many people who, despite believing in Jesus as their Savior, are yet to receive the remission of sin that can wholly cleanse their hearts as white as snow. These people are sinners, and therefore, the Holy Spirit cannot dwell in them. You must realize that those who believe in Jesus in this way believe in Him in vain. You must then also realize that the Holy Spirit comes to only those who believe in Jesus within the true gospel and are born again.

The Holy Spirit was sent to this earth after the resurrection of Jesus. When Jesus was on this earth in the New Testament's time, the Holy Spirit had not descended on the disciples yet. Jesus said, *"If anyone thirsts, let him come to Me and drink. He who believes in Me, as the Scripture has said, out of his heart will flow rivers of living water (John 7:37-38)."* And the Apostle John clearly interprets this, saying, *"But this He spoke concerning the Spirit, whom those believing in Him would receive; for the Holy Spirit was not yet given, because Jesus was not yet glorified" (John 7:39).*

As such, it was only after His Ascension that Jesus sent the Holy Spirit as He had promised (John 16:7). Acts 1:4-5 backs this interpretation: *"And being assembled together with them, He commanded them not to depart from Jerusalem, but to wait for the Promise of the Father, 'which,' He said, 'you have heard from Me; for John truly baptized with water, but you shall be baptized with the Holy Spirit not many days from now.'"* This was true that the Holy Spirit had not yet come to this earth and into the hearts of the disciples, up until the Day of first Pentecost in the Early Church period.

To whom, then, has Jesus given the Holy Spirit? He has given the Holy Spirit to those who believe in His baptism and the blood of the Cross, for this truth is the truth of the remission of sin. Jesus has given the Holy Spirit only to the saints and the Apostles who believed in the gospel of the water and the Spirit. The Holy Spirit is the hallowed Spirit of God. The word "holy" means "separated from sin." As such, the Holy Spirit cannot dwell in the hearts of sinners.

The disciples of Jesus were the ones who had followed Him and heard His Word while He was on this earth. They believed in Jesus as their own Savior and Lord who blotted out all their sins with His baptism and death on the Cross. The disciples also heard all that Jesus told them when He appeared before them after His resurrection: "You shall be baptized with the Holy Spirit." They believed that all their sins were passed onto Jesus when He, coming to this earth as their Savior, was baptized. Because Jesus was their Savior, He was baptized, shouldered the sins of the world, was crucified and died on the Cross, and thereby saved them perfectly from all their sins. Those who likewise believe together with the disciples in the gospel of the water and the Spirit have received the Holy Spirit as a gift.

We Receive the Holy Spirit as a result of Believing in the Gospel of the Water and the Spirit

Human beings can receive the Holy Spirit as a gift by believing in the gospel of the water and the Spirit. The Holy

Spirit, in other words, is a gift of God that He gives only those who have been forgiven of their sins. Let's assume for a moment that I gave a pair of sunglasses to someone as a gift, saying, "Enjoy your summer vacation! This is a small expression of my thanks for your help." If this person were to say to me, "I only have $10 right now, but here, have it for now," what would all this mean? It would mean that the sunglasses were not a gift but a good he just purchased. A gift is something that is given freely, 100 percent. If we had paid a price for it, no matter how small, then it is not a gift at all.

Because the Holy Spirit is given only to those have received the remission of sin, when people's sins disappear from their hearts by believing in Jesus, the Spirit of God then simultaneously and automatically comes into their hearts.

In short, the Holy Spirit is given to the born again the same time they truly believe in the gospel of the water and the Spirit. Jesus has perfectly saved those who believe that Jesus accepted all the sins of our entire lifetime passed onto Him when He was baptized, and that He bore all the punishment of sins by shouldering all our sins and all the worldly sins of mankind and being crucified. It is to those who believe in this that Jesus Christ gives the Holy Spirit as a gift.

Because the Spirit of God is a gift given to those who have received the remission of sin, all that people have to do is just accept Him. Because the Holy Spirit is a gift given to any saint who has received the remission of sin, He dwells in the hearts of the saints. Those who have the Holy Spirit in their hearts have the witness of the Word to the remission of their sins.

The Holy Spirit does not come in a hot and electrifying sensation. Nor is He felt emotionally. Far less does the Holy Spirit descend in the state of complete absence of ego as demons are summoned by witchcraft. Because the Bible says, *"Then there appeared to them divided tongues, as of fire, and one sat upon each of them,"* some of you may think and claim that a certain feeling arises when the Holy Spirit descends on you. However, you must know that such an experience is nothing to do with the Holy Spirit, but is merely the sign of being demon-possessed.

There used to be a professor at a seminary who claimed that when the Holy Spirit descends, He descends through the electrified hands. But this is not how the real Holy Spirit descends. You must therefore realize that if there is any spirit that comes into you like this, then this is not the Holy Spirit. Some people mistake demons descending on them as the Holy Spirit. They misunderstand and misbelieve these demons to be the Holy Spirit. When demons come in, people can feel them, but the Holy Spirit cannot be felt. The Holy Spirit quietly descends on us, together with the remission of sin, when we believe in the gospel Word of the water and the Spirit.

Absolute majority of today's Christians have not been born again by the gospel of the water and the Spirit even as they believe in Jesus somehow. They are still trying to receive the Holy Spirit after a few and even more years since they first believed in Jesus. But, you must realize it is wrong to try to receive the remission of sin and the Holy Spirit separately after believing in Jesus. Trying to receive the Holy Spirit separately after believing in Jesus, they climb up some mountain and pray, and do all kinds of crazy things in church, crying and wailing. These are all symptoms of the demon-possessed.

If we cannot receive the remission of sin once for all when we believe in Jesus, then we cannot receive the Holy Spirit separately later on. If people try to receive the Holy Spirit separately afterward without the gospel of the water and the

Spirit, they will be possessed by demons instead. Often, when people go to such places as prayer houses and fervently pray to God to give them the Holy Spirit, they do receive something. But what they receive is not the Holy Sprit, but demons that feign to be the Holy Spirit. You must realize that such happenings are frequent, and that you cannot try to receive the Holy Spirit without the gospel of the water and the Spirit.

To lead a biblically sane life of faith, one must believe in the gospel Word of the water and the Spirit. First of all, receive the remission of all your sins by the faith in the true gospel! You will then receive the Holy Spirit as a gift. When Jesus has blotted out our sins of the world with His water and blood, if you remain ignorant of this and only pray ardently to receive the Holy Spirit, you will then end up being seized by demons.

People misunderstand the gospel of the water and the Spirit, and just believe that Jesus has blotted out their sins only with the blood of the Cross. What would have happened had Jesus died on the Cross without first accepting all our sins passed onto Him through His baptism?

The Old and the New Testaments match with each other perfectly. In the Old Testament, sins were passed by laying hands on the head of a sacrificial animal. Likewise, God made Jesus take upon the sins of the world by being baptized by John. Had John not passed the sins of the world to Jesus through baptism, these sins would have still remained as they were, even until now. This is why like the Old Testament's laying on of hands, Jesus Christ had to take upon all the sins of the world by being baptized by John, the representative of mankind, prior to His being crucified. It was because Jesus Christ was baptized by John that He could go to the Cross and shed His blood.

Everyone must all believe in Jesus, who has blotted out

the sins of the world with His baptism and blood, and he/she must thereby be remitted of all his/her sins. Only when one's sins are remitted can he/she receive the Holy Spirit. If someone still has sin in his/her heart even as he/she believes in Jesus, then the Holy Spirit cannot dwell in this person's heart.

We Can Receive the Holy Spirit Only When We Have the Righteousness of God

The remission of sin and the Holy Spirit are not received separately. Those who are ignorant of this do not know the whole truth, and so they go to prayer houses or other such places, fast and pray. What do they do when they become too weak to finish that fasting? They think about Jesus' crucifixion and bear with their hunger, saying to themselves, "My hunger means nothing compared to Jesus' crucifixion!" There are many such people who are trying desperately to receive the Holy Spirit while living their spiritual lives with their sins remaining intact in their hearts.

What you must know clearly is that fasting per se is not what is important. What is truly important is to know and believe in the gospel of the water and the Spirit given by God and thereby have all your sins be remitted by faith. God wants you to know and believe in the gospel of the water and the Spirit more than to pray and fast with devotion. Why? Because this is what would bless you.

If someone prays, "Lord, give me the Holy Spirit," does the Holy Spirit then come to this person even when his/her heart still remains sinful? How can the hallowed Holy Spirit dwell in the hearts of the sinful? Only demons can dwell in such hearts of the sinful. Demons make the hearts of the sinful their houses, while the Holy Spirit makes temples out of and dwells eternally in the hearts of those who have received the remission of their sins by believing in the gospel of the water and the blood of Jesus Christ.

Sermon on the Holy Spirit 5

The Ministries of The Holy Spirit

< John 16:5-11 >

"But now I go away to Him who sent Me, and none of you asks Me, 'Where are You going?' But because I have said these things to you, sorrow has filled your heart. Nevertheless I tell you the truth. It is to your advantage that I go away; for if I do not go away, the Helper will not come to you; but if I depart, I will send Him to you. And when He has come, He will convict the world of sin, and of righteousness, and of judgment: of sin, because they do not believe in Me; of righteousness, because I go to My Father and you see Me no more; of judgment, because the ruler of this world is judged."

Let us examine what it is that the Holy Spirit does when He comes to this earth.

First, the Holy Spirit Convicts the World of Sin

The above passage tells us that the Holy Spirit convicts the world "of sin." Put differently, the Holy Spirit convicts people of their sin that leads them to hell. This sin is the sin of not believing that Jesus took upon all the sins of mankind once and for all by coming to this earth in the flesh of a man, and being baptized by John, all to save sinners.

By being condemned for the sins of mankind through the baptism of Jesus Christ and the blood of the Cross, God has saved you and me from our sins and punishment, and He has made us sinless.

The Holy Spirit convicts the world of not believing in this truth. It is the Holy Spirit who bears witness to the truth that not believing in the salvation of the water and the blood given by Jesus is the very sin leading to hell. And it is also the Holy Spirit who seals the born-again with the seal, "You are My children." This is how we came to call God as Abba, Father. It is because we have become sinless that we can call the Holy God as our own Father.

Second, the Holy Spirit Points out the Righteousness of God

Jesus said in the above passage, *"of righteousness, because I go to My Father and you see Me no more."* Jesus Himself is the very righteousness of God.

The "righteousness of God" has completed with Jesus' baptism and blood: Jesus Christ took upon all the sins of mankind by coming to this earth and being baptized, carried the sins of the world to the Cross, and atoned them perfectly by shedding His blood to death. The Holy Spirit testifies that Jesus has saved us through His baptism and blood.

The Holy Spirit therefore tells us, "Not believing in Jesus is the sin that leads people to hell. And that you have received the remission of sin—that is, that God has saved you with the water and the blood—is the very righteousness of God."

Third, the Holy Spirit Speaks of Judgment

Jesus continued to say in the above passage, *"Of judgment, because the ruler of this world is judged."* The Holy Spirit bears witness that Jesus Christ has judged the Devil with His perfect righteousness—His baptism and the blood of the Cross.

The Devil knew that Jesus was the Son of God. This is why he contrived to crucify Jesus. It was a work of Satan, who thought that killing Jesus would mean his victory.

Satan therefore incited people to crucify Jesus. Having thus been crucified, Jesus shed all the blood in His heart. Whenever the Heart of Jesus beat up, blood poured out of His vein. Right before His death, He cried out of thirst, put vinegar to His mouth, shouted out, "It is finished," and then died. And in three days, He rose from the dead again.

The works of the Holy Spirit are manifested through the righteous with the gospel of the water and the Spirit. Unfortunately, there are not that many people who have received the remission of sin by the works of the Word of the Holy Spirit's testimony at this point. Why? Because people have been deceived by the works of demons, and they have therefore been unable to be born again, receiving the spirits of demons and misbelieving them as the Spirit of Jesus.

That Jesus has saved us by coming to this earth, being baptized, dying on the Cross, and rising from the dead again—that means that He has made us righteous and will therefore take us to Heaven. This is what the Holy Spirit testifies.

Far too many people throughout the world still remain as sinners with sinful hearts even as they have believed in Jesus for 10, 20, or even 50 years. We can even see that for some people, the longer they have believed, the more they are bound by their sins. Having received the power of demons, they mistakenly think that speaking in tongues, which are nothing more than incomprehensible gibberish, and convulsive experiences, mean that they have received the Holy Spirit. But these are not the gifts of the Holy Spirit but of demons. It is, in other words, Christians being possessed by demons from their inability to discern the works of the Holy Spirit from the works of demons. The characteristics of the demonically possessed include convulsing violently, uttering incomprehensible words, rolled-up eyes and shaking bodies, and brazenly committing impersonal acts. The works of Satan makes people to live a life of faith that is extremely impersonal, with no intellect but only feelings and will.

The works of the Holy Spirit, in contrast, testify through the Word what is sin, what is righteousness, what is our salvation by God, what is His judgment, in which gospel we must believe to be saved, and who are the ones that will be condemned to hell.

Where is the evidence of your salvation from sin? You have been saved by believing in God's written Word of truth. It is because this Word of God is in your hearts that you have been saved for all your sins. But so many Christians cannot accept the true and beautiful gospel because there are lots of false teachings piled up in their mind previously. As there was no room in the inn to accommodate Mary who was pregnant with Jesus, such people must empty their hearts first to accept Jesus, and hold onto and believe in the written Word of God.

We must hold onto and believe in the gospel Word of the water and the Spirit, in the promise that Jesus Christ would come and save us. This is how we can be eternally saved from our sins and be approved by God the Holy Spirit. It is in the hearts of those who have become sinless by believing in Jesus that God the Holy Spirit can dwell. We have received the remission of sin, but we cannot but sin yet again. Of course, we do not sin willingly, but out of our weaknesses. No one can resist the temptation of stealing if he/she had gone three days without any food; likewise, we cannot avoid but sin always, but we still say that we have received the remission of our sins because we have the Word of God in our hearts.

This is why 1 Peter 3:21 says, *"There is also an antitype which now saves us—baptism,"* and 1 Peter 1:23 states, *"having been born again, not of corruptible seed but incorruptible, through the word of God which lives and abides forever."*

Before God, the Holy Spirit convicts people of sin, righteousness, and judgment. We have been saved from our sins by believing in the gospel of truth given by Jesus Christ. We believe that Jesus' baptism and His crucifixion are the love of God that has saved us sinners. And many people must receive eternal life by believing in the salvation that Jesus, who is the Judge, has given them.

Sermon on the Holy Spirit 6

Then You Shall Receive The Gift of the Holy Spirit

< Acts 2:38 >

"Then Peter said to them, 'Repent, and let every one of you be baptized in the name of Jesus Christ for the remission of sins; and you shall receive the gift of the Holy Spirit.'"

Do People Receive the Holy Spirit by Repenting?

What is the most biblically sound repentance? It is to receive the remission of one's sins by believing in the Word on the baptism and blood of Jesus.

No one can receive the remission of sins and become sinless before God through their devoted prayers of repentance. Moreover, it is even far less the case that they received the Holy Spirit by doing so. Receiving the remission of sin and the Holy Spirit is possible only for those who know and believe in the truth of the baptism and blood of Jesus. The Spirit of God comes as a gift to those who have received the remission of their sins.

The coming of the Holy Spirit to those who believe in Jesus is directly related to the remission of sin given by Jesus. Acts 2:38 states, *"Repent, and let every one of you be baptized in the name of Jesus Christ for the remission of sins; and you shall receive the gift of the Holy Spirit."* This gift is given "to you and to your children, and to all who are afar off, as many as the Lord our God will call (Acts 2:39)." What is critical in these passages is the relationship between the spiritual cleansing of sin and the blessing of receiving the Holy Spirit: God the Father made His Son accept the sins of the world passed onto Him, and it is by believing in this that we receive the remission of sin; and as a blessed result of this, we receive the Spirit of God as a gift. Have you received the Holy Spirit with such faith?

On the Day of the first Pentecost, the Apostle Peter preached to those who gathered around him that the resurrected Lord Jesus was the Savior of every one of them. Pay attention to the fact that they were Jews, who were well aware of the sacrificial system of the Old Testament. And most of them might see the crucifixion of Jesus about two months ago. Therefore, they could easily have faith in the gospel of the water and the Spirit when they were enlightened by the brief sermon that Peter had preached.

After hearing his teaching, they repented and confessed Jesus as their Savior. They all believed in Jesus' baptism and His death on the Cross, was cleansed of all their sin, and came to receive the Holy Spirit. Then, Peter baptized those who believed. Moreover, from here and on, as far as the Holy Spirit was concerned, the command to "wait" for Him was no longer repeated to those who have received the remission of sin. After the Day of Pentecost, receiving the Holy Spirit as a result of believing in Jesus no longer entailed any waiting; rather, when people believed in the baptism of Jesus and the blood of the Cross as their remission of sin, then they received the Holy Spirit the very moment they believed so.

Today's passage clearly supports that the faith that believes in the baptism of Jesus and the blood of the Cross is the condition to receiving the Holy Spirit after the events of the Day of Pentecost.

By repeatedly confirming the simple truth that the remission of sin was fulfilled by the baptism of Jesus, Peter concluded that the Holy Spirit was given as a gift to whoever believed in His Word of the gospel of the water and the Spirit, saying, *"For the promise is to you and to your children, and to all who are afar off, as many as the Lord our God will call" (Acts 2:39).* We should not miss the main stream that since the Holy Spirit was first mentioned in Acts 1, the baptism that Jesus received is the baptism that forgives all the sins of the world. The only condition of this "promise" in the Bible is to believe in the baptism that Jesus Christ received, the blood of the Cross, His death and resurrection. It is to those who believe in these that God has enabled them to receive the Holy Spirit.

The relationship between the faith in Jesus' baptism and God's gift of the Holy Spirit is such that the Holy Spirit is given only to those who have been washed of their sins by believing in the baptism and blood of Jesus. We must believe in this truth. The real truth that the Holy Spirit could come to this world is found in the fact that Jesus' baptism washed away the sins of mankind and His crucifixion bore the punishment of these sins. We must know and believe in the truth hidden in the remission of sin that enables us to receive the Spirit of God as the gift of salvation (Acts 2:38-41).

There are many debates going on among pastors and theologians about the indwelling of Holy Spirit. All kinds of different claims are made on how Christians can receive the Holy Spirit. But what we must remember here is that in the Bible, it is written that when people believe in the gospel of the water and blood of Jesus and of the Spirit, they receive the remission of their sins, and they also receive the Holy Spirit as a gift simultaneously. In short, the Holy Spirit infallibly comes to the saints whose sins have been forgiven.

For people to receive the Holy Spirit given by God, they must repentant in a biblically sound way. The true repentance is for people to turn around from rejecting God's unconditional love toward them. It is, in other words, to throw away all odds and ends that have stood against the true gospel, and to believe in the gospel of the water and the Spirit in heart. Only then can we receive the Holy Spirit as a gift.

The repentance with which we can receive the Holy Spirit is for us to turn around from disbelieving to believing in the gospel that enables us to receive the Holy Spirit. Everyone went on his/her own way and had stood against God. They all worshipped the creatures as their gods. When Jesus Christ, despite this, saved them from their sins with the water and the blood, far from believing in Him, they stood against the gospel that enables them to receive the Holy Spirit.

As such, in case of most Christians, the true repentance before God also means to return to the true gospel that enables them to be born again of water and the Spirit, turning around from their faith that believes only in the blood of the Cross. This is the true repentance that the Bible speaks of.

The Bible tells us, *"Repent therefore and be converted, that your sins may be blotted out, so that times of refreshing may come from the presence of the Lord" (Acts 3:19).* Likewise, the way for people's minds to be refreshed is to believe that Jesus has given them the remission of their sins through the baptism with which He accepted the iniquities of sinners and the blood that He shed on the Cross. To receive the Holy Spirit, all our sins must have been passed onto Jesus by believing in

Him and we must have no sin. And in our hearts we must believe in the Word that Jesus has given us salvation by taking our sins upon Himself, dying on the Cross, and thereby vicariously bearing all our condemnation in our place. This faith is the right faith of true repentance.

The Holy Spirit is the third Person of the Triune God. The son, the Father, and the Holy Spirit are all one God for us who believe in Jesus. Though they are each a different Person, they are nevertheless the same one God for us who believe in Jesus. Because the Triune God is the same one God for us, each of the Trinity planned together to save us from the sins of the world. And each of them works in their assigned ministries. As such, the Holy Spirit bears witness to the truth that Jesus Christ took upon all our sins of the world and was condemned vicariously in our place.

Acts 2:38 tells us that those who have receive the remission of sin *"shall receive the gift of the Holy Spirit."* Having planned to blot out the sins of the world, God the Father sent His Son to this earth. By being baptized to save sinners, Jesus the Son of God has given us the gospel that has made the sins of the world disappear. And now to those who believe, He made the Holy Spirit dwell in their hearts as God.

Those who have received the gift of the Holy Spirit are the ones who have been saved from all the sins of the world. Such people are God's children. They are the ones who have the Holy Spirit. As such, to receive the Holy Spirit, one must first turn around from all his/her own stubbornness that has stood against the truth. And, second, he/she must most certainly believe in the baptism and blood of Jesus as his/her own salvation.

Why does the Bible treat the baptism of Jesus so importantly? Because the baptism that Jesus received was absolutely necessary to blot out our sins. It was because Jesus had accepted all our sins passed onto Him through His baptism before being subjected to the punishment of crucifixion that He could die on the Cross in our place. In short, the baptism that Jesus received is important because it is through this that He took upon the sins of the world. Because the baptism of Jesus is the baptism of the cleaning of sin, faith in it is most required to receive the Holy Spirit, and it constitutes the gospel that enables us to receive Him. This is why Jesus' baptism is so important.

The Holy Spirit comes to us because we understand the reason why Jesus was baptized and believe in it. To turn our hearts sinless, we must listen to the Word of the baptism of that Jesus received and of the blood that He shed on the Cross. Only then can we receive the Holy Spirit given by the Lord. We must realize why Jesus, coming to this earth, had to be baptized. Only when we know this and then believe in the blood of the Cross can we have sinless hearts. Because Jesus came to this earth and washed away the sins of the world by being baptized, as a result of this He could pay all the wages of our sins on the Cross with His blood. This is why in our hearts we must believe in the baptism of Jesus and the blood of the Cross. Only then can we receive the gift of the Holy Spirit in our faith that believes in the gospel of the water and the Spirit.

The hearts of those who have received the Holy Spirit may not get too excited, but because they have the Holy Spirit in their hearts, they are refreshed automatically. As such, the hearts of those who have received the remission of sin are always joyful. The hearts of those who repent correctly are refreshed, for they infallibly receive the gift of the Holy Spirit at the same time as they receive the remission of their sins. And those who are born again receive their baptism unhesitatingly as the mark of faith that Jesus has saved them from all their sins through the Word of the water and the blood.

The Bible tells us that the people who were told about Jesus went through the kind of repentance that enabled them to become sinless. Have you gone through this repentance, the one that enables you to receive the remission of your sins and the Holy Spirit?

Sermon on the Holy Spirit 7

The Holy Spirit Fell upon the Gentiles

< Acts 10:44-48 >

"While Peter was still speaking these words, the Holy Spirit fell upon all those who heard the word. And those of the circumcision who believed were astonished, as many as came with Peter, because the gift of the Holy Spirit had been poured out on the Gentiles also. For they heard them speak with tongues and magnify God. Then Peter answered, 'Can anyone forbid water, that these should not be baptized who have received the Holy Spirit just as we have?' And he commanded them to be baptized in the name of the Lord. Then they asked him to stay a few days."

The biblical events surrounding Cornelius provide the answer to the question of whether or not it is by keeping the Law that one receives the Holy Spirit. They show us that those who received the Holy Spirit from God did not receive Him by keeping the law, but by believing in the gospel of the water and the Spirit.

That the Holy Spirit descended on Cornelius and his household shows us that this phenomenon is also related to their faith in the baptism and blood of Jesus. As such, the faith that could enable all the people in the world to receive the Holy

Spirit was only the faith that enables these people to receive the remission of their sins. Acts 11:17 also states, *"Therefore God gave them the same gift as He gave us when we believed on the Lord Jesus Christ...."* For the faith of Peter, receiving the Holy Spirit and receiving the remission of sin were the same. Therefore, the widespread belief in today's Christianity, that the faith that enables people to receive the Holy Spirit can be attained through the prayers of repentance, is a profoundly mistaken and completely fallacious belief. It is only by believing in the gospel of the water and the Spirit that we receive the Holy Spirit.

Seeing the Holy Spirit descending on Cornelius and his family, Peter said, *"Who was I that I could withstand God?"* (Acts 11:17) This means that the Holy Spirit comes to us as a result of believing in the baptism that Jesus received and in the precious blood of the Cross.

Acts 2:39 states, *"For the promise is to you and to your children, and to all who are afar off, as many as the Lord our God will call."* Now, people throughout the whole world have been enabled to receive the gift of the Holy Spirit by hearing the gospel of the water and the Spirit.

Sermon on the Holy Spirit 8

Test the Spirits to See Whether They Are from God

< 2 Thessalonians 2:7-12 >

"For the mystery of lawlessness is already at work; only He who now restrains will do so until He is taken out of the way. And then the lawless one will be revealed, whom the Lord will consume with the breath of His mouth and destroy with the brightness of His coming. The coming of the lawless one is according to the working of Satan, with all power, signs, and lying wonders, and with all unrighteous deception among those who perish, because they did not receive the love of the truth, that they might be saved. And for this reason God will send them strong delusion, that they should believe the lie, that they all may be condemned who did not believe the truth but had pleasure in unrighteousness."

Verse 7 from the above passage says, *"For the mystery of lawlessness is already at work; only He who now restrains will do so until He is taken out of the way."* This tells us that Satan spread the authority of the Devil by working with his own power (not the works of the Holy Spirit), something that God does not want.

Those who are seized by the lawless one are, to put it plainly, those who have "the faith of witches," not of Christians. These are those who devote themselves only to the gift of exorcism, other tongues, prophecies, healings, and other such works. They place more importance on what they claim to have seen, or what spiritual powers they claim to have received. But God said that He would end such works that block the truth.

2 Thessalonians 2:9-10 states, *"The coming of the lawless one is according to the working of Satan, with all power, signs, and lying wonders, and with all unrighteous deception among those who perish, because they did not receive the love of the truth, that they might be saved."*

The works of Satan are manifested, for example, among those who claim to have the power to heal. Some Christians, including pastors, church officers, and laymen, go to all kinds of meetings to fill their void of power, from special mountain prayer meetings to special charismatic movement meetings and special gatherings for the laying on of hands. Such people hang onto God earnestly, wailing and fasting before Him. Their purpose is to get their ministry approved by men, believing that proper ministering can come about only when it is accompanied by the kind of charismatic power that is shown in the Bible. But when people thus try desperately to be clothed in God's power, the Devil appears as Jesus and gives them his satanic power.

How Does the Mystery of Lawlessness Work?

Jude 1:11 states, *"Woe to them! For they have gone in the way of Cain, have run greedily in the error of Balaam for profit, and perished in the rebellion of Korah."* What, then, is the way of Cain? Cain went out from the presence of God after the Lord punished him. It was turning away from God. And turning against God is not believing in the gospel of the water, the blood and the Spirit given by the Lord.

Those who are seized by Satan work for money. The passage above continues, *"they... have run greedily in the error of Balaam for profit."* The pastors who are seized by Satan are ministering ultimately to make money. Imprisoned by Satan, they do the works of false prophets. These false prophets love it when their flocks bring in a great deal of money as their offerings to the church. They give their benediction for their flocks only when they cough up a lot of money, and when do they, then these false prophets do not bless them. Like this, those who minister while being seized by Satan are ministering ultimately for the sake of money.

If you hand out a lot of money, then they make you into a deacon or an elder as soon as possible. But if you do not cough up enough money, then you cannot become an elder at all.

The people to whom the above passage refers worked only for money. Who were they? The passage refers to Balaam, a prophet of the Old Testament, who led the people of Israel to fall into the secular world by selling them off for money. People who are like Balaam, and who work with the power of Satan, are the ones who work only for the sake of money.

The passage finally tells us that such people *"perished in the rebellion of Korah."* These people formed their own parties and stood against God's Church. People who love money will in the end turn into someone who stands against God.

Jude 1:12 states, *"These are spots in your love feasts, while they feast with you without fear, serving only themselves. They are clouds without water, carried about by the winds; late autumn trees without fruit, twice dead, pulled up by the roots."*

Those who see people only in monetary terms are geniuses in deceiving others and are expert in robbing their naïve followers of money. Because Satan's servants are the kind of shepherds who are only interested in feeding themselves, they do not think about the souls of the many at all. Even as people believe in Jesus, many of them are only exploited and have no peace of mind, with a constant anxiety over their sins and being driven insane by their worries.

Satan's servants are the charismatically inclined religionists who plant false faith with lies by receiving the power of Satan. And whenever these people speak about the Bible, they mix in lies, and they know no shame. Therefore, the Bible describes them as *"raging waves of the sea, foaming up their own shame"* (Jude 1:13).

When the end times of this world come, demons will work even more hard, and so the servants of Satan will also exercise more power. In the end times, before Jesus Christ returns, Satan will work forcefully even inside the churches on this earth. As such, demons will be run even more rampant then, driving out demons and prophesying.

What is the most important is for those who have not been born again even as they believe in Jesus to know and believe in the gospel of the water and the Spirit given by the Lord, and thereby receive the remission of sin and the gift of the Holy Spirit. And by having the Holy Spirit, they must have eternal life. But the self-styled servants of God who are seized by Satan seek after only the blessings of the flesh, the power to heal, speaking in tongues and experiencing miracles as their sole wish and purpose. This is why these people always front the weird experiences given by Satan.

In today's world, when someone starts to speak in other

tongues in one of the famous prayer houses, people around this person applaud him/her for doing so. And those who are unable to speak in tongues are especially gathered together in a room where they are taught by a trainer how to speak in tongues, repeating, "Lul-lu-lujah, Lul-lu-lujah, Hallelujah." When they try to utter this phrase faster, what they speak becomes incomprehensible gibberish, spewing out strange words as if running a bad recording tape (in trying to speak faster, people's tongues get all tied up). When 80 percent of them have already lost their reason and their tongues are all tied up, how could any of them pronounce correctly? It is because people receive the laying on of hands from the fanatics who are possessed by demons that they themselves become possessed as these demons move onto them and dwell in their hearts. It is because they are demon-possessed that they speak demonic words.

Do not be deceived by the works of demons, but believe that the true Holy Spirit works in the hearts and surroundings of those who believe in the gospel of the water and the Spirit written in the Bible. Even now, the lawless works of demons are unfolding among those who pursue charismatic faith.

But Even If You Repent on That Day

Matthew 7:22-23 also states, *"Many will say to Me in that day, 'Lord, Lord, have we not prophesied in Your name, cast out demons in Your name, and done many wonders in Your name?' And then I will declare to them, 'I never knew you; depart from Me, you who practice lawlessness!'"*

Many people believe that acting as a prophet in the name of the Lord, driving out demons, and doing wonders in His name are all the works of God and of the Holy Spirit. There are people in today's Christianity who claim that driving out demons is the work of the Holy Spirit, for many people believe that when wonders are brought to bear by some ministers, they believe all of them to be the works of the Holy Spirit.

But the Word says that such things are not the works of the Holy Spirit. It clearly records that such power of driving out demons, signs, miracles, and doing wonders are the works of Satan. Yet despite this, people believe them to be the works of the Holy Spirit. Satan's works come to those who are to be destroyed, and people who pursue such signs and miracles cannot be saved. Therefore, the Bible warns us, saying, *"Beloved, do not believe every spirit, but test the spirits, whether they are of God; because many false prophets have gone out into the world" (1 John 4:1).*

Sermon on the Holy Spirit 9

The Spirit-filled Life

< Ephesians 6:10-17 >

"Finally, my brethren, be strong in the Lord and in the power of His might. Put on the whole armor of God, that you may be able to stand against the wiles of the devil. For we do not wrestle against flesh and blood, but against principalities, against powers, against the rulers of the darkness of this age, against spiritual hosts of wickedness in the heavenly places. Therefore take up the whole armor of God, that you may be able to withstand in the evil day, and having done all, to stand. Stand therefore, having girded your waist with truth, having put on the breastplate of righteousness, and having shod your feet with the preparation of the gospel of peace; above all, taking the shield of faith with which you will be able to quench all the fiery darts of the wicked one. And take the helmet of salvation, and the sword of the Spirit, which is the word of God."

To be filled with the Holy Spirit, Ephesians 5:16-18 tells us, *"Redeeming the time, because the days are evil. Therefore do not be unwise, but understand what the will of the Lord is. And do not be drunk with wine, in which is dissipation; but be filled with the Spirit."*

For people to be filled with the Holy Spirit, they must first of all believe in the gospel of the water and the Spirit and live for this gospel. The reason for this is because one must have received the remission of sin first for the Holy Spirit to dwell in his/her heart, and one must have received the Holy Spirit for him/her to be filled with Him. In other words, the first priority for us is to become sinless in our hearts by wholeheartedly believing in the gospel of the water and the Spirit.

Second, we must redeem our time, for only those who redeem the time can serve the gospel faithfully and live their lives led by the Spirit.

Time does not wait for us forever. A week goes by in a blink of an eye. Going to bed after Sunday evening church service, we wake up in Monday morning. We talk with someone on the phone and meet someone, and the whole day is already gone by. When we think it's Tuesday, we are already into Wednesday. We attend Wednesday evening worship service, and then Thursday goes by, followed by Friday and Saturday, and in no time we are facing another Sunday. As such, it is only those who redeem the time and faithfully serve the works of this gospel can be filled with the Holy Spirit.

Third, those who know exactly what the will of the Lord is and serve this will are filled with the Spirit. Why? Because only when we know clearly what is the will of God in today's age is, can we finally make His will our objectives and do His works. We can do the works of the Lord led by the Holy Spirit when we are united with the Lord. If we live without knowing what the will of the Lord is, then we cannot avoid but live foolish lives. As such, to be filled with the Holy Spirit, we must know the Lord's will clearly.

Fourth, we must strive to gather together. We can be filled with the Spirit only if we strive to come together in God's Church, praise the Lord, and always thank God in the Lord's name. But those who neither listen to the Word of God and nor give thanks and praise to Him for the salvation and the works that the Lord has given them cannot be filled by the Spirit. The ones who can be filled with the Spirit are only those who always praise, thank, and strive to gather together in the name of Jesus Christ, as well as believe in God's will and Word manifested in His Church. As such, to be filled with the Holy Spirit, we must not miss our times of coming together.

When we hear the Word, it is important for us to hear it with our sincere hearts, not merely with our ears. And it is very important that we lead our lives of faith with our hearts. What we do without our hearts has nothing to do with the Lord, *"for man looks at the outward appearance, but the Lord looks at the heart" (1 Samuel 16:7).* As such, those who listen to the Word with their hearts can truly say "Amen" and be thankful. Also, because they can mediate on the Word that they heard, they can be filled with the Spirit. However, those who do not receive His Word with their hearts, even as they heard the same Word in the same meeting, they cannot say "Amen" and be thankful. The Holy Spirit is pleased by all our worship, praises, and prayers that are given to God with our sincere hearts.

For us to be filled with the Holy Spirit, there is no worldly shortcut. The only shortcut is to just believe in the Word of God and accept it into our hearts. This is why we must cherish our meetings and we must not regard them lightly. Only then can we be filled with the Spirit and defend our faith until the day of the Lord's return.

Fifth, those who believe in the Word of God are filled with the Spirit. When Ephesians 6:11 tells us to *"put on the whole armor of God,"* it is telling us that we must lead our lives of faith by believing in the Word of God. By hearing the Word of God spoken to us through His Church and believing in it, we can be filled with the Holy Spirit.

Sixth, we must hold onto the Word of God with our hearts. Ephesians 6:13 also tells us to *"take up the whole armor of God."* The word "take" here signifying an active faith. In other words, it is to read the written Word of the Bible and to hold steadfast in our hearts to what we have read.

The 66 Books of the Bible are filled with the Word of God. But no matter how abundant the Word is, if we do not hold onto it, then there can be no fullness of the Spirit. Regardless of how well we attend church and hear the Word, there are still many times when we become spiritually tired, empty and weary. There are many times when we somehow become weak. This is why we have to take the whole armor of God; that is, the Word of God. Even if it is just a single passage, if it is appropriate and necessary for you, then you must hold onto it. Holding onto the Word in your hearts in this way is none other than taking it, and this is the answer to living a life filled with the Spirit. And you must meditate on the Word, and live your lives by believing that everything will be fulfilled according to the Word. This is none other than the way to be filled by the Spirit.

In leading our lives of faith, if we do not hold onto the Word of God, then we cannot keep our faith. There are both good times and bad times when we lead our lives of faith in this world, and there are also times when our hearts sink low and become weak. In times like these, if we ourselves do not believe in the Word of God and hold onto it, then no one can encourage our faith. No one else can hold you steady. And even if someone were to hold you, your hearts cannot avoid but be always empty. As such, in such times, we must hold onto the written Word.

When you hold onto the Word of God, this Word holds

you steady and enables you to live immersed in the promised Word of God. Because the Word holds you, even if you are facing difficult circumstances or your thoughts go astray a bit, the Word wakes you up, making you return to your rightful place, live by faith, be immersed in the Spirit, and live a life that is filled with Him. This is why it is important for us to take the written Word of God.

When the people of Israel in the Old Testament were living in the wilderness, God brought down manna to them. Gathering manna and bringing them home, the Israelites cooked them in all kinds of different ways and ate them. Like this, among the countless written Word of truth, the Word of life, you and I hold onto the Word that is absolutely necessary for us, believe in it, and take it. When you do so, this Word then makes you pray, strengthens your faith, enables you to live in hope, and makes you serve the gospel. And it allows you to be blessed before God, to never leave Him but be near Him before His presence. It is, therefore, very important to take this Word to be filled by the Spirit.

The Faith in the Word of God Leads Us to the Spirit-filled Life

To reemphasize once again, it is those who believe in the Word of God in their hearts who can be filled with the Holy Spirit. When we hold onto the Word of God, when we believe in it and rely on it, the Holy Spirit who dwells in our hearts gives us faith and strength, approves our faith as right, and helps us at our side so that we can live our lives by believing in this Word. This is why He is called the Holy Spirit, the Helper or the Counselor (John 14:16).

As such, to be filled with this Spirit, the Bible tells us, *"Take up the whole armor of God, that you may be able to withstand in the evil day, and having done all, to stand. Stand therefore, having girded your waist with truth, having put on the breastplate of righteousness, and having shod your feet with the preparation of the gospel of peace; above all, taking the shield of faith with which you will be able to quench all the fiery darts of the wicked one. And take the helmet of salvation, and the sword of the Spirit, which is the word of God."*

Regardless of how weak your faith is and what your circumstances are, when you only believe in the Word of God and hold onto this Word, the Holy Spirit works forcefully in your lives and turns you into the people of faith. And when you are holding steadfast to the Word of God, the Holy Spirit strengthens you and thereby enables you to overcome Satan. He allows you to stand against Satan with your faith and transforms your surroundings.

When you are holding onto the Word of God, the Holy Spirit makes you pray, strengthens you, enables you to stand against the Devil when he attacks you, and empowers you to throw away every disbelief when it arises in your heart. Also, this Word makes you turn around from the errors of your faith, and it turns you into the people of faith like a rock standing firmly on the Word of God. As such, believing in and taking this Word is absolutely critical for you to be filled with the Spirit.

If you neither believe in nor take the Word, but only pray

blindly to be filled with the Spirit, you can never be filled by the Spirit in such ways. You must most assuredly hold onto the Word and take it. Only after doing so can you be filled with the Spirit by praying in Him.

From looking at these things, we can realize that being filled with the Spirit can come about only by believing in and taking the Word of God, discerning what the will of the Lord is and following this will by praying and redeeming the time, uniting together into the gatherings of God's Church, serving the Lord, and spreading the gospel. The Holy Spirit, of course, always helps us and works in our lives, but depending on whether we believe in the Word or not, and whether we hold onto it or not, the Holy Spirit either works forcefully or leaves us alone to our own strengths. As such, to be filled with the Spirit, we must think about the Word that tells us that the Lord has saved us, and we must have the joy of salvation by believing in this Word. We must believe in our hearts that spreading this gospel is the will of the Lord, and we must preach and serve it.

If you are the truly born-again righteous, then you must have had the experience of being inspired by the Holy Spirit when spreading the gospel, enabling you to speak the right words on the spot, and of your hearts being filled spiritually. As such, we must realize clearly that we cannot reach the fullness of the Spirit outside the Word of God, the will of the Lord, and the life in the Church, and that it can neither be attained by our own efforts.

In seeking to be filled with the Spirit, many of today's Christians blindly attend special meetings so-called "Tarrying Meetings," and in such meetings they pray, speak in the so-called tongues by making weird sounds, cry out the Lord's name, chant after slogans, and do all kinds of things trying to receive the Holy Spirit. But these are all completely foolish and groundless acts. The Holy Spirit is not someone who comes into our hearts just because we beg Him desperately. On the contrary, those who teach so and who try to be filled with the Spirit in this way end up being filled with the Devil instead. When we contemplate on, believe in, and take the Word and the will of the Lord that have saved us, and when we serve the gospel, we can then finally be filled with the Spirit. But we must remember that praying in our own emotions, overdriving ourselves, and doing all kinds of weird things will only result in being filled with the spirit of the Devil.

The Fullness of the Spirit Is Real

By now in the preceding discussion, we have what the fullness of the Spirit is, and I am sure you have full understanding on this topic. If we have a clear, intellectually sound understanding about the Spirit-filled life, we then take the Word with our hearts. We must hold onto the Word everyday, even if it is only a couple of passages. And we must ask ourselves what kind of the Word is necessary for our present circumstances, look for such Word, and then hold onto it in our hearts. This Word will then change our circumstances and transform our hearts. When this happens, our faith and hearts will mount up with wings like eagles, and run toward the will of the Lord without being weary, just as Isaiah 40:31 assures us, *"But those who wait on the Lord Shall renew their strength; They shall mount up with wings like eagles, They shall run and not be weary, They shall walk and not faint."* This is not just hypothetical, but it is real.

When we the born-again believe in the Lord in our hearts

and serve Him, consider church gatherings as precious and participate in them, and unite our hearts for the spreading of the gospel, then our hearts become filled with the Spirit naturally. We live, in other words, always immersed and filled with the Holy Spirit even without any particularly special effort. But what about people who are not like this? When such people do not unite with the gatherings or works of the church, they gradually move away from the church and eventually end up blaming and leaving it.

For you and I not to leave the Lord, regardless of how our acts and reflections are, and regardless of how great or small our faith is, all that we have to do is just grab the Word of God by believing in it unconditionally. Why? Because the power of the Word of God belongs to those who grab the Word steadfastly. This is why it is very important to take the Word of God. As such, we can be filled with the Spirit only when we live in this way.

We Must Not Be Drunk with the Wine of the World

Ephesians 5:18 states, *"And do not be drunk with wine, in which is dissipation; but be filled with the Spirit."* The "wine" here refers to all the things of the world. If we lose our hearts to the things of the world, then we cannot be filled with the Spirit. The lust of the flesh obstructs the desires of the Spirit. We the born-again can live only when we are filled with the Spirit. But the fullness of the Holy Spirit requires that we take the Word, and, as such, it is only when we thus take the Spirit that our lives as the righteous become worthy.

Not doing so, if we instead live drunk with the world half

the time and with the Spirit the other half the time, then there is no joy at all. Then, we would end up serving the gospel half-heartedly, and when we thus only go through the motion of doing the works of the Lord, not only do other souls remain unable to receive the remission of sin, but also our own lives of faith as the righteous become meaningless. This is why we must be filled with the Holy Spirit. We must live the Spirit-filled lives. Only then can we avoid leaving the Lord, and only then can we wholly receive the power that is found in this Word spoken by the Lord.

We Must Strive to Come Together with Psalms and Hymns

We must always believe in and live according to what Ephesians 5:19-21 tells us: *"Speaking to one another in psalms and hymns and spiritual songs, singing and making melody in your heart to the Lord, giving thanks always for all things to God the Father in the name of our Lord Jesus Christ, submitting to one another in the fear of God."*

Indeed we must. If we do not believe in the Word of God, how can we thank Him for our salvation, and how can we live by our faith? Also, even if we have already received the remission of our sins, if we do not hold onto the Word of the Scriptures all the time, how can we live with our hearts filled with the Holy Spirit? Such things can never happen. On the contrary, in our lack of faith we will easily be discouraged by small things that happen in everyday life, and even if we are touched by the Spirit while at the church, when something happens back home, our hearts will lose strength in no time. You and I must live only by believing in the Word of God.

We must live by serving the gospel in our lives, by believing in and taking the Word and praying. The Holy Spirit will then automatically help you, guide you, hold you steady, give you power and blessings, enable you to do the works of the Lord, to follow Him, and to stand against the Devil, and make everything work. Once you know it, being filled with the Spirit is very easy. I hope that each and every one of you would believe in the Word of God wholeheartedly.

The Holy Spirit Works in the Believers in God's Word

Contrary to what many people of today believe, the Holy Spirit does not come down while they just turn off all lights and cry out the name of the Lord incessantly. Why? Because the Holy Spirit always works in accordance to the Word.

To this very moment, I have never served the Lord in a big fuss. I have instead worked faithfully to the best of my abilities, believing in all the Word of the Lord in my heart and knowing His will. I do not try to achieve everything all at once either. Instead, I pray all the time, consult with other servants of God, and unite with them in one purpose, that is, serving the true gospel. When I reach a decision, I then make the necessary preparations, and to the best of my abilities I do the works of the Lord little by little. In no time, and without even realizing, I see that many things are then achieved. Preaching the gospel of the water and the Spirit has also been done in this way so far, and the Lord has worked forcefully in this endeavor. The works of the Lord are not achieved by following the dictates of some emotional sentiments, but they are implemented rationally and coolly by following the Word of God and believing in it in our hearts. Everything else that comes after that is all taken care of by the Holy Spirit then.

When kids do wrongs, their parents usually treat them coldly until they truly admit their mistakes. When even a human parent do so, wouldn't God the Holy Spirit rebuke us cold-heartedly when we go astray against the will of God? But, as soon as we repent of our wrongs, and thank God for perfectly saving the wrongdoers like us, He embraces and encourages us tenderly to keep on following His will.

What Must We the Spirit-filled Do?

The Lord tells us about the end of the age and the signs of the times, saying, *"nation will rise against nation, and kingdom against kingdom. And there will be famines, pestilences, and earthquakes in various places" (Matthew 24:7).* And he says that the Great Tribulation will soon follow these. It looks as though now is this time then, particularly when we look at natural disasters or the current political situation of the world. What is it, then, that we must do now? It is none other than obeying the Lord's command to spread the gospel of the water and the Spirit throughout the whole world.

We must then preach the gospel now, but we must do so by first asking God for the best possible method. We must not carry out this task tumultuously only with our strategy, strength and will, but the first thing that we must do is to pray to God to give us the faith and strength necessary to the spreading of the Lord's gospel, to strengthen all His people, to bless us both in our spirits and flesh, to allow us to serve the gospel, and to fill us with the Holy Spirit.

When we thus do what is feasible for us and gradually

expand the boundaries of our ministries, the Lord is pleased by us, and He will enable us to achieve great and many things in the future. Each of you will experience just how much our Lord actually holds and helps us, for we the righteous have already experienced for countless times that whenever we wanted to do something and prayed about it, it was actually fulfilled as intended. Does this then mean that we do such things out of our own strength? Of course not! In fact, we know nothing, but because God is pleased by what we do, we mount our challenge by faith, seeking His help, holding onto and taking the Word even more, and waiting in faith. One day, the Lord lets us to go to such and such places, and then we see that the workers and souls whom we have been looking for are waiting for us there.

For example, when we sought to preach the gospel overseas through literature, we needed people who could translate our books into different local languages. No matter how hard we looked, they were not easily found. But God made sure that the people whom we were looking for would have plenty of time to finish their training, and then had them ready for us when the time came.

We must realize that to follow the Lord and to be filled with the Spirit are not such difficult feats to achieve. We should realize that these things are very easy for those who have received the remission of sin, and that after thus receiving the remission of sin, God then works orderly, according to His Word, in the lives of those who believe in and take this Word. When we live immersed in the Word of God and His Church, the fullness of the Spirit comes about on its own accord.

What the born-again want is the fullness of the Spirit. Preach the Word and spread the gospel. You will then be filled with the Holy Spirit. When you serve the Lord with your hearts, you will be filled with the Spirit, and when you spread the gospel, you will also be filled with the Spirit. When you unite your hearts with the Church and live together, you can live a Spirit-filled life. This is very easy for those whose hearts are with the Church. But for those whose hearts are not united with the Church, there just is no way that they can ever be filled with the Spirit. Would the Holy Spirit come without any regard to the written Word of God? The Holy Spirit does not work outside God's Church and the works of the gospel.

How to Be Spirit-filled

First, those who want to receive the Holy Spirit must, above all, know and believe in the gospel of the water and the Spirit and thereby receive the remission of their sins.

Second, they need to have a clear and consecrated faith in the truth that God gives the Holy Spirit to only those who have received the remission of sin, even now from the Apostolic Age and on (Acts 2:38).

Third, their hearts must turn away from the sin of not believing in the Word of the Bible and from their disbelief.

Fourth, to receive the Holy Spirit, their souls need to be taught with the concrete Word. As such, they need to listen carefully to the blessed Word of being born again of water and the Spirit, and when needed more, they should share the gospel fellowship personally with the servants of God and receive the Holy Spirit. The Holy Spirit will then make them believe in the Word of God in their hearts, be born again, and receive Him. But if they try to receive the Holy Spirit without any discernment by blindly giving prayers of repentance or trying to live a life of self-holiness, or if they unconditionally yearn after the Holy Spirit and attempt to receive Him through self-injurious and fanatical fasting or mountain prayers, they will only end up falling into great confusion.

We must remember that the Spirit of God is not given just because people want to receive Him on their own, but He comes to only those who are ready to receive Him. The Holy Spirit does not come to those who give mountain prayers, participate in a charismatic meeting, or pursue only gifts, all on their own. If you think that you received something akin to the gift of the Holy Spirit while participating in such meetings or from your own beliefs, there is something else that you must think of first. And this is whether or not there are sins in your hearts. If there are sins in your hearts, then you must realize that what you had received is not from the Holy Spirit, but from the Devil, and you must cast it out. We must first realize where and in whom the Holy Spirit truly works.

There is something that we must not forget in seeking to receiving the Holy Spirit. This is to believe equally in both the baptism of Jesus (Matthew 3:15) and His blood of the Cross. The Holy Spirit is independent, but He comes only to those who believe in the baptism of Jesus Christ and the blood of the Cross as the remission of their sins. As such, the Holy Spirit comes to and works in the lives of those who believe in the gospel of the water and the Spirit as their true salvation.

The Gifts of the Holy Spirit

When we look at the Bible, we can see that the gifts of the Holy Spirit are mentioned in several places. Representative of such lists of gifts are found in Romans 12:6-8, 1 Corinthians 12:8-10, and Ephesians 4:11. But today, we will look at the nine gifts listed in 1 Corinthians 12.

1) The gift of the Word of knowledge: This is the knowledge of the mysteries of the gospel of the water and the Spirit that is hidden, in accordance to the special providence of God, in the Word of the Bible written by the inspiration of the Holy Spirit. The ability to clearly explain and spread this gospel of the water and the Spirit is the very gift of the Word of knowledge.

2) The gift of the Word of wisdom: The gift of the Word of wisdom does not refer to human wisdom, such as one's brightness or intellect. This gift of wisdom is the gift of solving the various issues raised by people by explaining the Word of the Bible with faith.

3) The gift of faith: The gift of faith is the gift of having action-oriented faith in the Word. This kind of gift is given when we hear the Word of God, and then believe in this Word with pure faith. The Holy Spirit works so that faith in the Word of God would rise in the hearts in the saints. With this gift, God also enable us to save people's souls from their sins.

4) The gift of healing: Instead of trying to heal the sicknesses of the flesh, the saints must realize that the will of the Lord is for them to know the providence of God from their illnesses, to obey this providence, and to heal spiritual illnesses rather than the illnesses of the flesh. The Lord advises us to pray for the healing of the sick (James 5:14-15), and such prayer is a prayer that every saint can give.

5) The gift of the working of miracles: This refers to the power of faith that believes in and follows the Word of God. Miracles refer to the faith that believes in the Word of God that defies the laws of nature known to us in general. Such a faith of the saints enlivens and empowers their lives of faith, enabling them to bear even more fruits. God makes the saints act by

faith.

6) The gift of prophecy: This is believing in the Word of God and spreading it on His behalf. Through the Old and New Testaments, God has already revealed to us His will and plan. As such, those who prophesy can most certainly prove the correctness or fallacy of such prophecies through the already written Word of God. Those who do not spread the Word of God written in the Scriptures by faith are false prophets. The rightful prophecy is spreading the Word of God by faith. By preaching to people the written Word, the saints and servants of God must enable them to worship Him, and to edify, exhort, and comfort each other. Jesus Christ has given, along with His body, the Church, the gift of faith that believes in the Word to the servants of God.

7) The gift of discerning of spirits: The discerning of spirits is the ability to discern whether people have received the remission of their sins or not just by hearing what they say. For us who are now living in the end times, if we do not have this gift, we would then risk being deceived by the Devil (1 Timothy 4:1). With this gift, we can discern those who seek after and follow only the gifts of the Holy Spirit, and can distinguish the born-again from those who have not yet received the remission of sin and the Holy Spirit.

8) The gift of tongues: When it is said that the saints speak in tongues, it means that they speak the truth of the Kingdom of Heaven. When the saints are praying to God in a personal setting, it is possible for them to speak in tongues, which can be understood only by God. But rather than trying to speak in tongues, we must put more efforts into understanding the Word of the Bible. We must realize that we would rather speak five words with our understanding to teach others than ten thousand words in a tongue (1 Corinthians 14:19).

9) The gift of the interpretation of tongues: This is the ability to teach the will of God for everyone's understanding by interpreting the Word given by Him. This gift of the interpretation of tongues was given in the Early Church period for the sake of spreading the gospel, and now it can be found in the ministry of translating and interpreting the gospel teachings. If one can speak in local languages, he/she would need no interpreter, but those who face the barriers of the many languages of the world can work through interpreters.

The Fruits of the Holy Sprit

"But the fruit of the Spirit is love, joy, peace, longsuffering, kindness, goodness, faithfulness, gentleness, self-control. Against such there is no law" (Galatians 5:22-23). The fruits of the Spirit are manifested as shown in the above verse.

Love: Love is the heart of Jesus. All the commandments and laws of God can be summarized as "to love God and to lover each other." But, we should remember that prior to our love for God, God first loves us unconditionally. His love is revealed in the Word of the gospel of the water and the Spirit, the Word that delivers everyone from sin and makes him/her God's own child. Those who receive the love of God through the true gospel sufficiently can have the heart of Jesus, that is, the love.

Joy: This is the indescribably glorious joy that arises from the depth of our hearts when our souls are born again by believing in the salvation of the remission of sin. This is why Paul, having received the remission of sin, could be joyful even in prison, and the saints of the Early Church could also rejoice.

There is joy in the hearts of the righteous who have received the remission of sin (Philippians 4:4).

Peace: Peace fills those who have received the remission of sin, which is invincible at any circumstances. There cannot be peace in the hearts of those who are afraid of God's Judgment for their sins. But it is the peace of our minds that have received the remission of all our sins once for all, as white as snow, by believing in the gospel of the water and the Spirit. The gospel of the remission of sin enables us to overcome our fear of sins, and it gives us the conviction of salvation and strong courage. Also, those who bring peace are approved as the children of God (Matthew 5:9), enjoy the joy of having received the remission of sin (Proverbs 12:20), and live a righteous life (James 3:18).

Longsuffering: Starting with our faith in the Word of being born again and of the remission of sin given by God, and with the strength of His Spirit, we bear the fruits of longsuffering in all things. These fruits of longsuffering are found in the hearts of those who have been saved by believing in the gospel Word of the water and the Spirit, and they can be attained from our long fellowship with the Holy Spirit.

Kindness: Kindness refers to understanding others and kindly teaching them the Word of truth. This entails a heart that has compassion for other souls, just like the merciful grace of God that has saved sinners through the baptism of Jesus and the blood of the Cross.

Goodness: Goodness means being virtuous and decent. Matthew 12:35 states, *"A good man out of the good treasure of his heart brings forth good things, and an evil man out of the evil treasure brings forth evil things."* For those who have become righteous before God, the fundamentals of their hearts are good and meek. So when we look at the people who have become righteous by faith, we can see their essential goodness and meekness in the depth of their hearts.

Faithfulness: Faithfulness refers to the faith that does not ever change under any circumstances but serves the gospel without fail. Faithfulness here entails "faith" and "loyalty." As such, only those who have received the remission of sin by believing in the gospel Word of the water and the Spirit given by Christ can be faithful to God.

Gentleness: Gentleness is a heart that completely understands others and that obeys the will of God. The gentle are the ones who pray even for their enemies who stand against them.

Self-control: Self-control refers to the ability to keep oneself under control. In particular, it refers to the ability to restrain, rein in, and control over the sinful and corrupted lusts of the flesh that run against the Holy Spirit. In other words, it means to live a life that is prudent, without self-indulgence, and under control. It goes without saying that we need self-control over bad things, but even when it comes to good things, we must always have self-control.

The Spirit-filled Life

We cannot live the Spirit-filled life by our own will or effort, but it is possible by Christ who lives in us (Galatians 2:20). We believe that our bodies have now become the instruments that are used to fulfill the will of Christ. Our minds have the thoughts of Christ, our will is ruled by the will of the Lord, and all our character and abilities are given to Him as offerings without any exception—living in this way is living a life that is filled with the Spirit. This is not a life of spiritual poverty, defeat and despair, but it is a life of constant victory, joy and affirmation that has the power to save the world through the gospel of the water and the Spirit (Romans 8; Acts 17:6). The characteristics of the Spirit-filled life can be summarized as the following.

It is a life that is always thankful for the joy of receiving the remission of sin (1 Thessalonians 1:6-7), and that pursues the righteousness of God as well. Those who rejoice with the will of the Lord are those who have been filled with the Spirit. Those who are overjoyed with the spreading of the gospel of the water and the Spirit are the ones whose lives are filled with the Spirit. Those who believe in, follow, and obey the written Word of truth lead their lives with the fullness of the Spirit.

The Results of Being Filled with the Spirit

"But you shall receive power when the Holy Spirit has come upon you; and you shall be witnesses to Me in Jerusalem, and in all Judea and Samaria, and to the end of the earth" (Acts 1:8).

• The faith of power: Those who believe in the gospel Word of the water and the Spirit receive the right to become God's children (John 1:12). The power that is given to us as the children of God is the power to overcome our sins and to carry out the will of God in this world. It is the authority to control over the demon-possessed and to save them with the gospel of the water and the Spirit. It is the authority to heal spiritual illnesses (Mark 16:18), to overcome the curses of Satan (Luke 10:19), to enter into Heaven (Revelation 22:14), and to live by believing in all God's Word of promise (2 Corinthians 7:1).

• The faith of victory: The Holy Spirit is the Spirit that

solves our problems. In this world and in our lives, there are countless problems that cannot be solved on our own (Zechariah 4:6-7). Even Christians cannot escape from the reality of the countless problems that life brings to them. But when we are filled with the Spirit, we can have such problems solved as the following and live a life of victory.

First, we can overcome the temptations of the world. The Holy Spirit enables us to decisively overcome and triumph over the temptations and enticements of sin that approach our hearts ceaselessly.

Second, we can solve the problem of death through the Holy Spirit. When we are filled with the Spirit, we can boldly overcome the endless fear and dread of death. Spirit-filled Christians can look toward the hope of Heaven and can more than overcome the problem of death (2 Corinthians 5:1).

Third, when we are filled with the Spirit, we can love, with the gospel of the water and the Spirit, even those whom we cannot possibly love on our own, and reach our happiness.

Fourth, we can be freed from the life of curse brought by Satan through the Holy Spirit. By believing in the remission of sin given by Christ and the fact that that we have now become His children, we can triumph, through the Holy Spirit, over the fear and terror brought by Satan.

Fifth, the Holy Spirit enables us to overcome all kinds of despair. When Elijah fell into despair, he regained his strength by hearing the voice of the Word of God, and when the disciples of Jesus fell into despair, they also rose up again by believing in the Word of God and only through the power of the Holy Spirit. Likewise, when we become filled with the Spirit by believing in the written Word of God, we, too, are more than able to rise up from the dejection and despair of our lives (John 14:16-18).

Above all, the Holy Spirit is the witness of the gospel of the water and the Spirit. As such, if one is a saint filled with the Spirit, the greatest interest for him/her is to live a life that testifies Christ' gospel of the water and the Spirit. The Holy Spirit does not give us mystical gifts or transcendent experiences. If you think that the Holy Spirit led you into mystical experiences, then this is not the work of the Holy Spirit but of the Devil.

The Day of Pentecost, therefore, is the very birth date of the Church. In this light, the Spirit-filled Christians use all their strengths to plant God's Church, to serve it and to expand it. The result of being filled with the Spirit is to live a life that testifies and serves the gospel of the water and the Spirit given by God.

Maintaining the Fullness of the Spirit Continuously

1) The born-again must cast aside their greed of the world. And they must take the Word of faith and truth (Ephesians 6:17).

2) Read and believe in the Word of God (Hebrews 4:12).

3) Gather together in the Church everyday (Hebrews 10:25).

4) Confess your sins and have faith in the gospel of the water and the Spirit (Psalms 51:4-5, 11-13).

5) Follow the desires of the Holy Spirit (Galatians 5:16).

6) Do not grieve the Holy Spirit (Ephesians 4:30).

7) Do not quench the gifts of the Holy Spirit (1 Thessalonians 5:19).

8) Stay away from the hearts of the flesh, and believe in

and spread the gospel Word of the water and the Spirit (Proverbs 4:23; Philippians 4:13).

9) Live a life that unites with God's Church and spreads the gospel of the water and the Spirit at every opportunity. You will then be able to maintain a life that is always filled with the Spirit.

Put differently, to be Spirit-filled we have to receive the holy Spirit first, and to receive the Holy Spirit, we must first cast out our sins that weigh our hearts down. This is the utmost important condition to receive the Holy Spirit.

Acts 2:38 states, *"Then Peter said to them, 'Repent, and let every one of you be baptized in the name of Jesus Christ for the remission of sins; and you shall receive the gift of the Holy Spirit."* Proverbs 28:13 also states, *"He who covers his sins will not prosper, But whoever confesses and forsakes them will have mercy."* To wash away our sins, we must first believe in the baptism of Jesus and His blood, and thereby be cleansed of all our sins.

We must believe in the power of the water baptism of Jesus and be baptized in faith. Matthew 3:16 states, *"When He had been baptized, Jesus came up immediately from the water; and behold, the heavens were opened to Him, and He saw the Spirit of God descending like a dove and alighting upon Him."*

Believers receive their baptism as the mark of their faith that believes that all the sins of the world were passed onto Jesus when He was baptized. As such, those who believe according to the Word of the Lord must be baptized. Let us never disobey God by refusing to be baptized, thinking of baptism only as a formality.

Of course, to be Spirit-filled, we must pray to God by believing in Him. Jesus said in Luke 11:13, *"If you then, being evil, know how to give good gifts to your children, how much more will your heavenly Father give the Holy Spirit to those who ask Him!"*

To all the saints gathered at the Mount of Olives just before His ascension, Jesus told them not to leave Jerusalem but to wait for the Holy Spirit permitted by the Father. The saints obeyed His Word and accordingly gathered together and prayed in an upper room in Jerusalem, and when the Day of Pentecost arrived, suddenly the Holy Spirit filled them all, descending on them like a rushing mighty wind and divided tongues of fire.

There is something that we must pay particular attention here. This is the fact that while there had been 500 brothers who had heard the Word of the Lord and witnessed His ascension, there were only 120 who actually prayed to Him in obedience to His Word.

To maintain the Spirit-filled life, we must spread the gospel of the water and the Spirit incessantly.

In Matthew 7:11-12, our Lord said, *"If you then, being evil, know how to give good gifts to your children, how much more will your Father who is in heaven give good things* [the Holy Spirit] *to those who ask Him! Therefore, whatever you want men to do to you, do also to them, for this is the Law and the Prophets* [the core teachings of the Scriptures]*."*

Water must be flown; if it remains stationary in one place, it will corrupt eventually. Likewise, those of us who have received the grace of the Holy Spirit with the remission of sin must devote ourselves to spreading the gospel of the water and the Spirit.

Faith in the Holy Catholic Church

The Apostles' Creed's confession of faith "in the Holy Spirit" is followed by its confession of faith in "the holy catholic Church." Here, the word 'catholic' refers not to the Roman Catholic Church, but to the universal church of the Lord Jesus Christ.

The Apostles, who believed in the baptism and blood of Jesus, witnessed Jesus Christ to many people on the Day of Pentecost. Then, they came to repent, and also believed in the baptism of Jesus, and become saints, and thereby the Church was established for the first time. As such, those who believe in the works of the Holy Spirit also believe in the Church, which has been established by these works of the Spirit.

What Kind of Church is God's Church?

In the original Scriptural texts, the word "church" is "ἐκκλησία" *(Ekklesia)*, meaning "the gathering of the called out." In other words, this refers to the gathering of those who believe in the baptism and blood of Jesus, in the truth that He has given them salvation.

God's Church is the gathering of those who believe in the truth that Jesus has saved sinners with the baptism that He received and the blood that He shed on the Cross. God distinguishes between the Church that He Himself found and others that have nothing to do with Him. The Church that was founded by God is one that was established to give the blessings of the remission of sin to all people. As such, the Church founded by God does not teach the ethics and morals of mankind, but it teaches Jesus' baptism of the remission of sin, the blood of the Cross, and salvation. The Lord has therefore permitted His Church to those who believe in the gospel of the water and the Spirit. Mere mortals cannot undermine this Church, nor can even Satan prevail against it (Matthew 16:18). God alone rules over His Church, guides it and works in it.

The gathering of the sinless saints who have been saved by believing in the gospel of the water and the Spirit is God's Church (1 Corinthians 1:2), and it is therefore a place where His special love and protection is found (Romans 8:35-39). As such, God blesses those who serve His Church and punishes those who persecute it.

The expression "holy Church" implies that all the believers who belong to the Church are the sinless ones who have received the remission of their sins by believing in the baptism and blood of Jesus, and the gathering of such people is called God's holy Church. **Therefore, to take part in God's holy Church, one must first believe in the gospel of the water and the Spirit.**

In the holy Church, the saints worship God by offering thanks, glory, and praise to God within the faith that believes in the gospel of the water and the Spirit, and by believing in His Word.

The fundamental meaning of the worship that we give to God is to adore Him by believing in the gospel Word of truth that has saved sinners from all their sins and iniquities. Only those who believe in the baptism of Jesus and the blood of the Cross as their own salvation are the true worshipers to God.

In God's Church, the sermons of the gospel of the water

and the Spirit are proclaimed ceaselessly. As such, we must give our worship to God with our faith, within this gospel of the water and the Spirit that is testified in God's Church.

The true worship given to God, therefore, is a worship of individual faith in the true gospel, not a worship inspired by a religious atmosphere. The true worshipers always worship God in spirit and in truth (John 4:24). As Hebrews 10:25 states, *"Not forsaking the assembling of ourselves together, as is the manner of some, but exhorting one another, and so much the more as you see the Day approaching."*

It is by the baptism of Jesus and the blood of the Cross that we are cleansed of all our sins. Human beings must admit that their existence is, because of their original and personal sins, like a pile of filthy manure. But even this filthiness is made clean when covered by snow. Likewise, when we believe in the baptism of Jesus and the blood of the Cross as our own salvation, we can then become sinless. Because Jesus has already atoned all our sins with His baptism and His blood of the Cross, and because He has thus made us righteous, if we only believe in this, we can all receive the remission of our sins and become righteous. This is why 1 Corinthians 1:2 states, *"To the church of God which is at Corinth, to those who are sanctified in Christ Jesus, called to be saints, with all who in every place call on the name of Jesus Christ our Lord, both theirs and ours."*

We believe that we have become righteous by believing in the baptism of Jesus and the blood of the Cross as the remission of our sins, and that it is by this faith that we are to enter Heaven. Anyone who believes in this truth can enter the Kingdom of God, no matter who he/she may be, whether from the East or the West, man or woman, old or young, rich or poor, privileged or underprivileged, knowledgeable or ignorant.

A balloon vendor was floating white balloons into the air. A black girl approached him and asked, "Can black balloons also float up to the sky?" The vendor answered, "of course." Whoever believes in Jesus true gospel can enter Heaven. There is no difference (Romans 3:22; Galatians 3:28). But before God, no one who has sin in his/her heart can ever ascend to Heaven. Even if one believes in Jesus somehow, if he/she still has sin, then this person just cannot ascend. However, because God has already forgiven all the sins of mankind with the gospel of the water and the Spirit, anyone who knows and believes in Jesus correctly can enter Heaven. Why? Because he/she no longer has any sin. Anyone who believes in the baptism that Jesus received from John and the blood of the Cross as the salvation from all his/her sins can enter Heaven by faith.

When Jesus takes our souls to Heaven, this is made possible because we have no sin anymore. Our Lord is omnipotent. As such, the beginning, the process, and the result are all the same. Our deeds are imperfect until the day we enter His Kingdom. But the works of the Lord, His baptism and the blood of the Cross, is perfect forever, and have made us holy. This is why Ephesians 1:4 says, *"Just as He chose us in Him before the foundation of the world, that we should be holy and without blame before Him in love,"* and 1 Thessalonians 5:23 states, *"Now may the God of peace Himself sanctify you completely; and may your whole spirit, soul, and body be preserved blameless at the coming of our Lord Jesus Christ."*

Faith in the Communion of Saints

What Is the Communion of Saints?

Those who received the salvation from all their sins by believing in the truth that Jesus is God Himself, and in the baptism that He received and the blood of the Cross, are the ones who have joined the family of God. As Ephesians 2:19 states, *"Now, therefore, you are no longer strangers and foreigners, but fellow citizens with the saints and members of the household of God."* The righteous have fellowship with each other.

There Is a Precondition to the Communion of Saints with God

Before we hold communion with the other saints, there must first be the communion with God. This is why the latter half of 1 John 1:3 states, *"Truly our fellowship is with the Father and with His Son Jesus Christ."*

That's right! There must first be the communion with the Lord. For there to be the communion with the Lord for us, we must first receive the remission of our sins by believing in the gospel Word of the water and the Spirit that He has given us. Why? Because the Lord is the Holy One who is sinless.

Those who thus have the right relationship with the Lord first by receiving the remission of sin can have the right fellowship with the other righteous persons as well. The saints who have been saved through the baptism and blood of the Lord can have fellowship with God, on their above, and, at their sides, with their fellow saints. The God-given salvation enables us to have fellowship with God, and with the fellow saints as well. In other words, because of the works of the baptism of Jesus and the precious blood of the Cross, we, who had been God's enemies before, have now come to serve Him as our own Father by first being forgiven of all our sins. And furthermore, we have to come to forgive, understand, and have fellowship with one another when we admit the works of Christ that has perfectly removed the blockages among us.

The Core Essence of the Communion of Saints Is the True Gospel and True Love

By giving the righteousness of the salvation of His baptism and His bloodshed of the Cross to those who believe, Jesus declares, "You have now received the remission of your sins." The One who thus told us is the Lord. And He admonishes us to love the Lord, and to live with the fellow saints in peace also. The Apostle Peter, who had disobeyed the Lord before but was forgiven, explained his joy by saying, *"And above all things have fervent love for one another, for 'love will cover a multitude of sins'" (1 Peter 4:8).*

That's right! As trees and grasses grow when watered, and the saints grow by the fellowship with each other, by the Word, and by the love of God.

From Acts 2:46-47, we can see the beautiful lives that saints of the Early Church had lived: *"So continuing daily with one accord in the temple, and breaking bread from house to house, they ate their food with gladness and simplicity of heart, praising God and having favor with all the people. And the Lord added to the church daily those who were being saved."*

Not every Christian who professes to believe in Jesus actually believes in the true Jesus. This means that those who do not know the gospel of the water and the Spirit given by Jesus, and therefore do not believe in it, are not saints. As such, the true forgiveness and fellowship can only be possible within the gospel of the water and the Spirit.

Ecclesiastes 4:9-12 states, *"Two are better than one, because they have a good reward for their labor. For if they fall, one will lift up his companion. But woe to him who is alone when he falls, For he has no one to help him up. Again, if two lie down together, they will keep warm; But how can one be warm alone? Though one may be overpowered by another, two can withstand him. And a threefold cord is not quickly broken."*

Let us all put our efforts into the communion of saints, looking at ourselves to see if any of us has been left alone and ostracized.

The works and burdens you have to bear may be too much for you. Then, you have to share your problem with you fellow saints, for *"you are not able to perform it by yourself"* (Exodus 18:18). And Matthew 18:20 states, *"For where two or three are gathered together in My name, I am there in the midst of them."*

There is an orient saying, "When there is peace in the family, everything is fine." Taking a step further, we can say, "When there is peace among the saints in God's Church, everything indeed is fine." When the saints are at peace with God, everything works out. It is when we first have peace with the Kingdom of the Lord that we can have peace in our homes and with each other.

Faith in the Forgiveness of Sins (1 John 1:9)

We believe that only the Lord can wash away our sins with the gospel Word of the water and the Spirit. As such, Isaiah 1:18 states, *"'Come now, and let us reason together,' Says the Lord, 'Though your sins are like scarlet, They shall be as white as snow; Though they are red like crimson, They shall be as wool.'"* In 1 John 1:9, it is also said, *"If we confess our sins, He is faithful and just to forgive us our sins and to cleanse us from all unrighteousness."*

Here, we must realize that the phrase "if we confess our sins" does not mean that God forgives our sins whenever we give prayers of repentance. Rather, 1 John 1:19 exactly means that we receive the remission of all our sins when we admit our sinfulness before the Lord and believe that the Lord has already blotted them out with all the sins of the world through the baptism that He received and the blood of the Cross. Anyone who admits his/her sins before God and believes in the gospel of the water and the Spirit is clothed in the grace of the remission of sin by God.

What Are the 'Sins' Here?

Every descendant of Adam is born with sin. Therefore, no one can claim to be "sinless" by not committing any sin, for human beings, having originally been born with sin, already have sin even if they do not commit any sin. As such, everyone needs the Savior who can save him/her from sin. Those who claim to be sinless and to have no need to believe in Jesus only end up standing against God.

At the beginning, God created the heavens and the earth, made the Garden of Eden, and allowed Adam and Eve to live in it. In this place where there was no sin, God had the most familiar fellowship with them in personal relationship. But to make them His children, God had given them a law. This law was not to eat the fruits of the tree of the knowledge of good and evil. God had said to them, "for in the day that you eat of it you shall surely die." And to give them eternal life and everlasting blessings, God told them to eat the fruits of the tree of life. But instead of eating the fruits of the tree of life as God had told them to, they ate the fruits of the tree of the knowledge of good and evil, the tree that would lead them to their certain death (Genesis 2:17, 3:22).

Falling into the Devil's temptation, Adam and Eve ended up eating the forbidden fruits of the tree of the knowledge of good and evil. Death came as the price of this sin. This is why Romans 5:12 states, *"Therefore, just as through one man sin entered the world, and death through sin, and thus death spread to all men, because all sinned."* As such, human beings now came to need their Savior.

Some people are self-confident, like the rich young man in Matthew 19, that they have kept all the commandments of God since their childhood. But there is no one who has ever kept all the 613 commandments of God.

Then why God gave us the Law, which we cannot observe at all. The Bible says that through the law we become conscious of sin (Romans 3:20). The Ten Commandments that God has given us point out our sins. For instance, someone might hate his/her own parent, thinking in his/her minds, "That old guy must be senile!" This person is then already breaking the Fifth Commandment of God's Law. And when a man lusts after a woman in his thoughts, even if he does not actually commit adultery, he has already broken the Seventh Commandment. Moreover, God also considers covetousness, jealousy, and hatred as murder even if we do not actually kill someone, for these are what motivate us to murder. Who, then, can ever completely keep the clear and spotless commandments of the Law of God that pierce through the deepest recess of our thoughts?

Furthermore, James 2:10 states, *"For whoever shall keep the whole law, and yet stumble in one point, he is guilty of all."* In this light, who can possibly claim to be sinless before this strict Law of God?

In our weaknesses, we often stumble in sin. Why is this the case? It is because of our original sin—that is, it is because human beings are fundamentally corrupted. This is why David, repenting from his sin of breaking the Seventh Commandment, said in Psalm 51:5, *"Behold, I was brought forth in iniquity, And in sin my mother conceived me."* David, in other words, admitted his fundamental sin. The prayers of repentance offered by the ordinary Christian today and David's confession of himself as fundamentally a mass of sins are completely different from each other. The former only admits one's actual sins of deeds, while the latter, in contrast, admits that he cannot help but sin because he is fundamentally a mass of sins.

Only those who recognize their fundamental selves as big masses of sins and believe in the gospel of the water and the Spirit given by the Lord can receive the grace of the remission of sin from God. Wouldn't this be the case? What is the right thing for us to do? Is it to list our daily sins before God and ask for His forgiveness everyday, or is it to recognize our weaknesses, admit our true selves as big masses of sins, and believe, in thankfulness, in the gospel of the water and the Spirit given by the Lord? The latter, of course, is the right thing for us to do! Let us all believe that by knowing and believing in the gospel of the water and the Spirit, we can have all the problems of our sins solved away.

In John 6:53-55, Jesus said, *"Most assuredly, I say to you, unless you eat the flesh of the Son of Man and drink His blood, you have no life in you. Whoever eats My flesh and drinks My blood has eternal life, and I will raise him up at the last day. For My flesh is food indeed, and My blood is drink indeed."* Here, that we must eat the flesh of the Lord and drink His blood means that that we must have the faith that believes that Jesus took upon all the sins of the world with the baptism that He received from John. This means that if we do not know the truth of the baptism of Jesus, then we cannot pass our sins onto Him, and our sins therefore cannot be forgiven, either. If we have been running a tab at a store, then we would remain debtors until we pay off the tab completely. Likewise, if we say that there was no baptism that Jesus received from John, the representative of mankind, when He came to this earth, then nor can we say that our sins have been forgiven (Matthew 3:15, 11:11-13).

The crucifixion of Jesus was a consequence of the fact that before this, He had first taken upon the sins of mankind through the baptism that He received from John. As such, the Lord has saved us from our sins by being crucified, shedding His precious blood, and thereby bearing all the condemnation of our sins for our sake.

When we profess to believe in Jesus, we must believe that He took all our sins upon Himself with His baptism.

The Bible speaks clearly about the believers' remission of

sins, which can be summarized into two main points. First, it tells us that by being baptized, Jesus accepted all the sins of the world passed onto His body.

Psalm 32:1 states, *"Blessed is he whose transgression is forgiven, Whose sin is covered."* The word 'atonement' contains the meaning of 'to take upon sins' and 'to accept sins.' As such, 1 Peter 3:21 says, *"There is also an antitype which now saves us—baptism (not the removal of the filth of the flesh, but the answer of a good conscience toward God), through the resurrection of Jesus Christ."* With baptism that He received from John, Jesus accepted all the sins of everyone in this world once and for all.

Second, the Bible tells us that Jesus has blotted out our sins.

Isaiah 43:25 says, *"I, even I, am He who blots out your transgressions for My own sake; And I will not remember your sins."* "To blot out" here means to make it disappear by painting over and to blow away like powder.

This means God the Father has cleansed away the sins of the world by passing them onto His Son through His baptism. For those among us who might be saying, "I have no hope since I've committed so many sins," they, too, can be freed from all their sins by hearing the Word of the gospel of the water and the Spirit. The Devil says to us, "Haven't you committed all kinds of sin?" But even if we had heard such words, when we believe in the baptism of Jesus and the blood of the Cross, then we can all be liberated from all such sins. When we have this kind of faith, the Devil gets scared and runs away. We are convinced that the Lord has forgiven our sins with the baptism and blood of Jesus. When we believe that Jesus has forgiven all our sins with His baptism and the blood of the Cross, then His amazing works of peace come into our lives. This is the central faith of Christianity, the faith of the remission of sin.

The Result of Receiving the Remission of Sin

It is to be freed from our sins and our fear of death. When people do not believe in the gospel of the water and the Spirit, they are abandoned by God, and therefore they are plagued by many tragedies and worries, unable to avoid their terrifying death. As such, human beings have done their utmost to be saved from their sins and death. Sometimes they turned to the so-called religious rituals made by their corrupted selves, continuing to cling to their repentance, asceticism and meditation, all to no avail. But to us who believe in Jesus as our Savior, His baptism and blood have not only forgiven us of the sins of the world, but they have also restored our relationship with God that had heretofore been broken, and have thereby freed us from our sins and our fear of death.

Everyone who believes in the gospel of the water and the Spirit has consistently made such a confession. With His baptism and blood, the Lord has forgiven even people like myself of all my sins. Until we have this kind of conviction, our hearts are weighed down and worrisome. But the believers who have been forgiven of their sins by believing in the baptism and blood of Jesus come to rejoice in the grace of the remission of sin, the likes of which they had never experienced before in this world.

Looking at us, who had been sinners before but who now believe in the baptism of Jesus and His bloodshed on the Cross, the Lord has washed away our blemishes, forgiven us of all our heavy sins, and thereby given us true peace. As the Lord has purchased our bodies by paying for them with His own precious blood, in thankfulness we remain faithful to Him, saying, "What shall I render to the Lord for all His benefits toward me? " (Psalm 116:12)

Faith in the Resurrection of the Body

No matter who, everyone dislikes hardships, is averse to illnesses, laments aging, and are scared of death that would approach them at their end. This is because sufferings, illnesses, and death, which were not supposed to have come to mankind, nevertheless sprung up as the wages of sin.

Fundamentally speaking, because of the sin of the father of mankind, human beings have been driven away from everlasting happiness. This is why people endlessly seek after their lost eternal life and yet are unable to reach it because of their sheer incapacity, looking at it as if it were an unattainable picture and ultimately succumbing to their death in the end. This is why all human beings come to seek after their salvation from someone other than themselves, confessing, *"O wretched man that I am! Who will deliver me from this body of death?"* (Romans 7:24) The answer to this cry is the last part of the Apostles' Creed—that is, it is the confession of faith in the resurrection of the body and the life everlasting.

Matthew 16:26 says, *"For what profit is it to a man if he gains the whole world, and loses his own soul?"* Given this, the issue of the resurrection of the body and the life everlasting cannot but be much more important than any other issues of politics, economy, education, sports, diplomacy, military, or modernization. Why? Because these things are earthly issues of a lifetime that lasts no more than a hundred years, and they cease to be issues as soon as one departs from this world. Therefore, it is the resurrection and the everlasting life that are the greatest issue of our lives.

Before we consider this issue, let us first address the problem of death for a while.

Those who seek the final answer to the problem of death are the wise, for without knowing the last direction of life, no one can find the way to the true life.

The dead do not move. The dead can neither hear nor see. For them, their knowledge, wisdom, fame, wealth, power, as well as everything else, no longer have any meaning—that is, such things become nothing to them. If cremated, their bodies turn into ashes, and if buried, they rot away under the ground. Death is the most horrible event that everyone faces. But the horror of death disappears in the power of salvation that Jesus has given us. This truth is found in the gospel of the water and the Spirit.

In Luke 8:52, Jesus said, *"Do not weep; she is not dead, but sleeping,"* and He then raised Jairus' daughter. Jesus saw the death of the chosen—that is, of the believers—as their separation from God physically and for a while. However, He declared that they would live again by believing in the gospel of the water and the Spirit.

In the first half of Matthew 10:28, Jesus also said, *"And do not fear those who kill the body but cannot kill the soul,"* telling us about the immortality of human souls. As such, Jesus Himself entrust His own soul to the Father when He passed away, and all the saints that preceded us have also done so when they left this world behind (Acts 7:59).

In What Kind of Body Do We Live Again?

Life is everlasting. Since the creation of the universe, life has never ceased to exist but has continued to live. Life has neither volume nor weight, but it has a great strength. A tree's roots can break through rocks and turn it into a great tree. Its life draws water from the ground and makes leaves and fruits, for life is the strength itself. Although death is strong and it seems invincible, what is even stronger than death is life.

The believers have received the Spirit of Jesus into their hearts when they believed in His baptism and blood as their salvation from their sins. As such, 1 Peter 1:23 states, *"having been born again, not of corruptible seed but incorruptible."* When the time comes, this seed of life will most certainly perform the work of resurrection. Romans 8:11 therefore says, *"But if the Spirit of Him who raised Jesus from the dead dwells in you, He who raised Christ from the dead will also give life to your mortal bodies through His Spirit who dwells in you."*

What, then, is the nature of the resurrected body? The Bible speaks about this in several places, but the clearest and most detailed explanation is provided in 1 Corinthians 15:42-44: *"So also is the resurrection of the dead. The body is sown in corruption, it is raised in incorruption. It is sown in dishonor, it is raised in glory. It is sown in weakness, it is raised in power. It is sown a natural body, it is raised a spiritual body. There is a natural body, and there is a spiritual body."*

The nature of the resurrected body, therefore, is fundamentally different from the nature of the earthly body, for it will be like the resurrected body of Jesus Himself. This is why Philippians 3:21 tells us that Christ *"will transform our lowly body that it may be conformed to His glorious body."*

That is exactly right! The salvation spoken of by Christianity is not only of our souls, but it is also of our bodies. Let's now examine this fact in more detail.

Our bodies will be transformed into incorruptible bodies. The nature of our earthly bodies is corruptible. As 1 Peter 1:24 states, *"All flesh is as grass, And all the glory of man as the flower of the grass. The grass withers, And its flower falls away."* It is also said in 2 Corinthians 4:16, *"our outward man is perishing,"* and Proverbs 31:30 states, *"Charm is deceitful and beauty is passing."* No matter how youthful and beautiful our bodies may be, they will all eventually decay away.

But the resurrected body is transformed into an incorruptible body. As Jesus ate in His resurrected body, so shall we. Some may question, then, whether or not we would have to deal with waste, since we would be eating in our resurrected bodies. But there would be no waste, for our bodies would have been made new, so would everything in the entire universe have been renewed, and therefore nothing would be corruptible anymore. Therefore, in the immortal realm of Heaven, where we will be living in our resurrected bodies, we will enjoy food, but there will be no decay, no stench, and no pollution whatsoever—a world, in short, that is perfectly clear and clean.

Our bodies will be transformed into strong bodies. It is often said that depression, no matter how severe, never hits hospitals, pharmacies, and funeral homes. This is a frank expression that reveals the sheer weakness of human beings. We die from our illnesses ravaged by unseen germs, or from our injuries suffered in accidents.

But the resurrected body is the indestructible body that suffers from neither illnesses, nor injuries, nor even from death. As the three saints of Shadrach, Meshach, and Abed-Nego who emerged unscathed from the fiery furnace burning seven times hotter than it was usually heated (Daniel 3:19-26), our resurrected bodies will be utterly strong. Like this, the lives of the saints in Heaven will see no illness, nor injury, nor death, for they will be living in a paradise filled with healthy joy and happiness.

Our bodies will be transformed into spiritual bodies. This does not mean that our bodies will be changed into spirits, but that they will be liberated like our spirits. While in this world, our bodies are slow and inconvenient. But the resurrected body is limited neither by time nor by space. It will be freed, as the resurrected Jesus appeared before His disciples with no temporal or spatial constraints, going through closed doors, appearing and disappearing all of a sudden. This is the spiritual body.

Who, then, are the ones who will receive this blessing? They are the ones who believe in Jesus as the Savior within the gospel of the water and the Spirit. John 11:25-26 therefore states, *"Jesus said to her, 'I am the resurrection and the life. He who believes in Me, though he may die, he shall live. And whoever lives and believes in Me shall never die. Do you believe this?'"* And John 20:29 also says, *"Jesus said to him, 'Thomas, because you have seen Me, you have believed. Blessed are those who have not seen and yet have believed.'"*

Death is tragic and horrible. But if we believe in the atonement of the baptism and blood of Jesus, then we will all be saved from our sins, freed from the fear of death. We will become the ones who live in this hope, preaching this gospel directly and indirectly.

Faith in the Everlasting Life

This declaration, which we believe "in the everlasting life," is the last confession of faith in the Apostles' Creed, and at the same it is our highest and greatest hope.

There are some people who say that the world is such a miserable place that they would be better off the sooner they die. But such is merely a complaint what is quite far from their real mind. Most people do not want to die, and even though this world is indeed full of troubles, they would still like to live a long life. Why is this so? Because as Ecclesiastics 3:11 says, God *"has put eternity in their hearts."*

Everyone has the desire to eat. And to satisfy this desire, there are all kinds of food available to them. People also do not want to live alone, but they instinctively long for the opposite sex. This is why there are men and women. Like this, the reason why people have the instinct to seek after eternity is because there is eternal afterlife.

It seems as though while people believe in the immortality of their souls, only a few believes in the immortality of their flesh. But with the advancements in science, we have come to discover the law of constancy of mass, that is, while materials may change in their forms, in their substance they do not change.

Water, for instance, remain in its liquid form in room temperature, but when the temperature drops, it solidifies into ice, and if heated, it vaporizes into gas. But this does not mean that the water itself disappeared, but only that it had changed in its form.

Like this, when our bodies of the flesh die, they turn into ashes if cremated, and they decompose if buried under the ground. But these are only chemical changes. In other words, after death our bodies do not disappear completely, but they only change in form, and their composing elements still remains intact.

In particular, for the flesh and spirits of Christians, simultaneous to their passing away, their souls are completely sanctified and ascend to Heaven, while their bodies remain without senses until the day of the Lord's return. When the Lord comes back, the dead are resurrected, the resurrected are transformed, and they then live forever, with their souls and bodies reunited, in the Kingdom of the Father. Jesus therefore said in John 11:25-26, *"I am the resurrection and the life. He who believes in Me, though he may die, he shall live. And whoever lives and believes in Me shall never die."* As such, the everlasting life of human beings is never a dream, but it is real and true. Those who have become sinless by believing in Jesus will indeed live forever.

God is the God of love and justice. He therefore blesses the good and punishes the evil. But in this world, the rewarding of the good and the punishment of the evil are not actualized properly. Why? Because human beings have not been made to live only in this world and then cease to exist with death, but they have been made to live forever in the next world.

This is why Jeremiah, a servant of God, asked Him, *"Yet let me talk with You about Your judgments. Why does the way of the wicked prosper? Why are those happy who deal so treacherously?" (Jeremiah 12:1)* Jeremiah then followed his questions by saying, *"Pull them out like sheep for the slaughter, And prepare them for the day of slaughter."* He believed, in other words, in the afterlife judgment, and answering his own questions.

As Jesus said in Matthew 25:46, *"And these will go away into everlasting punishment, but the righteous into eternal life,"* there is no mistake that human beings live not only in this world, but also forever in their afterlife.

What Is It Meant by Souls Receiving Eternal Life?

This means to live with God forever. Only the sole living God of the Father, the Son, and the Holy Spirit, who have been and will be forever, has eternal life. As such, the true meaning of eternal life is to take part in God's life.

That's right! What makes Heaven a paradise for us is the fact that God, the root of all blessings, will be with us. It is a place where only those who have received the remission of sin by believing in the baptism and blood given by Jesus will be living. Revelation 21:3-4 therefore state, *"And I heard a loud voice from heaven saying, 'Behold, the tabernacle of God is with men, and He will dwell with them, and they shall be His people. God Himself will be with them and be their God. And God will wipe away every tear from their eyes; there shall be no more death, nor sorrow, nor crying. There shall be no more pain, for the former things have passed away.'"* That's right! If there is such a thing as eternal life without God, it can only be the everlasting suffering of hell. There is no greater blessing than the fact that God is with us forever. We sing the old hymn, "Jesus, the very thought of Thee; With sweetness fills my breast; But sweeter far Thy face to see. And in Thy presence rest."

It means a life of happiness that lives forever. Christ now has restored the everlasting life that we had lost because of the failure of Adam, our forefather, to keep his covenant and his inability to eat the fruits of the tree of life, and He has given us eternal life. In Revelation 22:1-2, John testifies, *"And he showed me a pure river of water of life, clear as crystal, proceeding from the throne of God and of the Lamb. In the middle of its street, and on either side of the river, was the tree of life, which bore twelve fruits, each tree yielding its fruit every month."*

"Living on the shore, I'm living on the shore, I'm living where the healing waters flow; Living on the shore, I'm living on the shore, I'm living where the healing waters flow."

It means eternal life without any sin. Because of the religious corruption that has led to the persecution of Christians by idolaters and their oppression by atheists, because of the political corruption that has led to the tyranny of the powerful and unbridled slander and backstabbing, and because of the moral corruption that has led to the endless flow of obscenity, fraud, theft, robbery, violence, and murder, this world remains constantly volatile.

But the everlasting life in the next realm of Heaven is lived in a domain where such evils are all eliminated, and which is filled with only peace and righteousness. Hence, 2 Peter 3:13 states, *"Nevertheless we, according to His promise, look for new heavens and a new earth in which righteousness dwells."*

Because God will eliminate not only the evils of this world but also our remaining corruption, we will all live in the happiness of eternal life in the Heaven of peace, where sin will no longer trouble us.

Only those who have been born again of water and the Spirit can enjoy such eternal life. Words cannot describe the sheer beauty and glory of Heaven, and so the Bible only describes them to us symbolically. Revelation 21:2 describes Heaven as *"prepared as a bride adorned for her husband,"* and verse 11 tells us that it has *"the glory of God,"* whose *"light was like a most precious stone, like a jasper stone, clear as crystal."* Verse 18 says that *"the construction of its wall was of jasper; and the city was pure gold, like clear glass,"* and verse 21 states that *"the twelve gates were twelve pearls: each individual gate was of one pearl."* The bride's adornment, precious stones, pure gold, and pearls—all these things describe the best in earthly terms, for there is no other way to describe Heaven better.

Let's say that one of your acquaintances climbed a famous mountain. When you ask him how the experience was, he might say, "I can't even begin to describe how beautiful it was! It was so amazing that no word can ever describe it!" When words fail us to describe even a mountain, how could they ever describe the eternal glory of Heaven?

It means eternal life having fellowship with God in perfect intellectual faculty. As 1 Corinthians 13:12 states, *"For now we see in a mirror, dimly, but then face to face. Now I know in part, but then I shall know just as I also am known."* We will know and have perfect fellowship with not only those whom we had been personally acquainted with while on this earth, but also with those who had come before us and those who would come after us, without even being introduced to them. This fact is proven by the passage in Matthew 17:1-8, where Peter, seeing Moses and Elijah appearing when Jesus was transfigured, said, *"Lord, it is good for us to be here; if*

You wish, let us make here three tabernacles: one for You, one for Moses, and one for Elijah" (Matthew 17:4). This shows us that Peter was able to immediately recognize Moses and Elijah, each of whom had lived over 1,500 years and 800 years before Peter's own time.

Do we have parents, husbands, wives, brothers, sons and daughters who had lived in faith and went to God before us? When this time comes, we will meet them again in joy, and there will be no more separation. Believers do not exist only ephemerally and then disappear. Those who have received eternal life by believing in Jesus will have both their souls and bodies saved, and they will live with the Lord forever.

It can only be a great blessing that we are able to confess our faith with the Apostles' Creed, the same Creed in which the saints before us had believed in and confessed. Why? Because those affirm and confess the Apostles' Creed as their own faith and follow it with an "Amen" are the blessed ones who will live forever in the beautiful Kingdom of Heaven.

In conclusion, Jesus spoke of knowing and believing by integrating them together. He said some very difficult and mysterious Word: *"You must eat My flesh and drink My blood. Only then can you receive eternal life."* How important is this Word? It tells us of the relationship between our souls and the life of Christ, like the flesh needing to eat and drink. This is the Word that tells us to believe in the fact that Jesus, through the baptism that He received from John, took all the sins of the world upon His own body. And it is telling us to believe that He died on the Cross, and that He rose from the dead again in three days.

The promise of God is a gift. It is not something that we can receive with our own works or penance. As such, we must believe in the Word of Christ, obey it and be faithful to it.

There is the Word of life that follows this. Because we know about eternal life, we must embark on the narrow path. We must keep on following the will of God, no matter how lonely it would be. We must walk on the narrow way even though we lose everything for that.

This is the way of those who receive eternal life. This eternal life can be attained through our voluntary death, as it is written, *"He who loves his life will lose it, and he who hates his life in this world will keep it for eternal life" (John 12:25).* And its beginning is none other than this very moment, right now. The beginning of eternal life is not after our death, but now. We must realize this. Today, when we live with Christ, marks the beginning of eternal life. A life that overcomes death, that triumphs over sin, and that is faithful to Christ—this in itself is the everlasting life.

We will live in eternal life. We will live forever. The water of life taught by the Bible is all found in the gospel of the water and the Spirit. Those who believe in this gospel of the water and the Spirit also believe in the everlasting life. Hallelujah! I praise our Lord! You, too, must believe in the Lord who has come to us of the water and the blood.

The Holy Spirit rebukes people of their sins. He makes them realize that all human beings are under sin as the descendants of Adam and Eve, and that they are evil beings who cannot avoid but face their death because of the sins that they commit everyday. But when people believe in the baptism and blood of Jesus, the Holy Spirit also guarantees their salvation.

Moreover, the Holy Spirit also bears witness to the righteousness of God. He condemns as sinners, rebukes, and punishes those who do not believe in the gospel of the remission of the sins of mankind that Jesus has fulfilled—that is, in the baptism and blood of Jesus as their remission of sin.

The Works of the Holy Spirit in Those Who Have Been Born Again

He makes the saints to keep their holiness.

He teaches and leads the saints and the servants of God.

He comforts and helps them. In our lives, sadness and suffering approach us endlessly. Coming to us who have been hurt, the Holy Spirit heals us and comforts us. Not only this, but He also helps us in our weaknesses and strengthens us.

Romans 8:26 states, *"Likewise the Spirit also helps in our weaknesses. For we do not know what we should pray for as we ought, but the Spirit Himself makes intercession for us with groanings which cannot be uttered."*

Like this, the Holy Spirit works in the hearts of the saints. For both the Apostles and us, we all have one Lord, one faith, and one baptism (Ephesians 4:5). Hallelujah!

I praise the Lord forever for giving us the faith of the Apostles. ⌧

HAVE YOU TRULY BEEN BORN AGAIN OF WATER AND THE SPIRIT?

HAVE YOU
TRULY BEEN
BORN AGAIN
OF WATER AND
THE SPIRIT?

PAUL C. JONG

Among many Christian books written about being born again, this is the first book of our time to preach the gospel of the water and the Spirit in strict accordance with the Scriptures. Man can't enter the Kingdom of Heaven without being born again of water and the Spirit. To be born again means that a sinner is saved from all his lifelong sins by believing in the baptism of Jesus and His blood of the Cross. Let's believe in the gospel of the water and the Spirit and enter the Kingdom of Heaven as the righteous who have no sin.

RETURN TO THE GOSPEL OF THE WATER AND THE SPIRIT

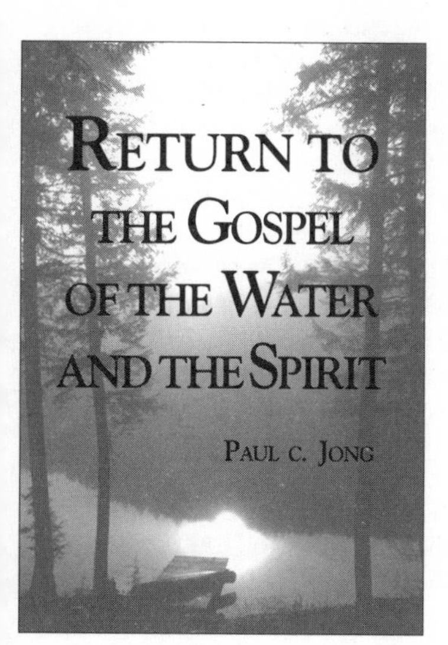

Let's return to the gospel of the water and the Spirit. Theology and doctrines themselves can't save us. However, many Christians still follow them, and consequently have not been born again yet. This book clearly tells us what mistakes theology and doctrines have made and how to believe in Jesus in the most proper way.

The Fail-safe Way for You to Receive the Holy Spirit

In Christianity, the most significantly discussed issue is salvation from sins and the indwelling of the Holy Spirit. However, few people have the exact knowledge of these two topics. Nevertheless, in reality people say that they believe in Jesus Christ while they are ignorant of true redemption and the Holy Spirit.

Do you know the true gospel that makes you receive the Holy Spirit? If you want to ask God for the indwelling of the Holy Spirit, then you must first know the gospel of the water and the Spirit and have faith in it. This book will certainly lead all Christians worldwide to receive the Holy Spirit through the remission of all their sins.

Our LORD Who Becomes the Righteousness of God (I) & (2)

The teachings in these books will satisfy the thirst in your heart. Today's Christians continue to live while not knowing the true solution to the personal sins that they are committing daily. Do you know what God's righteousness is? The author hopes that you will ask yourself this question and believe in God's righteousness, which is dealt in detail in these books.

The Doctrines of Predestination, Justification, and Incremental Sanctification are the major Christian doctrines, which brought only confusion and emptiness into the souls of believers. But, dear Christians, now is the time when you must continue in the Truth which you have learned and been assured of.

These books will provide your soul with a great understanding and lead it to peace. The author wants you to possess the blessing of knowing God's righteousness.

IS THE AGE OF THE ANTICHRIST, MARTYRDOM, RAPTURE AND THE MILLENNIAL KINGDOM COMING? (I)

After the 9/11 terrorist attacks, traffic to "www.raptureready.com," an Internet site providing information on the end times, is reported to have increased to over 8 million hits, and according to a joint survey by CNN and TIME, over 59% of the Americans now believe in apocalyptic eschatology.

Responding to such demands of the time, the author provides a clear exposition of the key themes of the Book of Revelation, including the coming Antichrist, the martyrdom of the saints and their rapture, the Millennial Kingdom, and the New Heaven and Earth-all in the context of the whole Scripture and under the guidance of the Holy Spirit.

This book provides verse-by-verse commentaries on the Book of Revelation supplemented by the author's inspired sermons. Anyone who reads this book will come to grasp all the plans that God has in store for this world.

IS THE AGE OF THE ANTICHRIST, MARTYRDOM, RAPTURE AND THE MILLENNIAL KINGDOM COMING? (II)

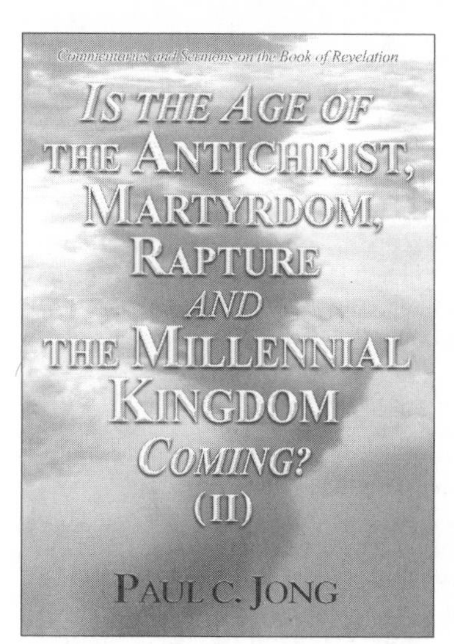

Most Christians today believe in the theory of pre-tribulation rapture. Because they believe in this false doctrine teaching them that they would be lifted before the coming of the Great Tribulation of seven years, they are leading idle religious lives steeped in complacency.

But the rapture of the saints will occur only after the plagues of the seven trumpets run their course until the sixth plague is all poured-that is, the rapture will happen after the Antichrist emerges amidst global chaos and the born-again saints are martyred, and when the seventh trumpet is blown. It is at this time that Jesus would descend from Heaven, and the resurrection and rapture of the born-again saints would occur (1 Thessalonians 4:16-17).

The righteous who were born again by believing in "the gospel of the water and the Spirit" will be resurrected and take part in the Rapture, and thus become heirs to the Millennial Kingdom and the eternal Kingdom of Heaven, but the sinners who were unable to participate in this first resurrection will face the great punishment of the seven bowls poured by God and be cast into the eternal fire of hell.

The TABERNACLE: A Detailed Portrait of Jesus Christ (I)

How can we find out the truth hidden in the Tabernacle? Only by knowing the gospel of the water and the Spirit, the real substance of the Tabernacle, can we correctly understand and know the answer to this question.

In fact, the blue, purple, and scarlet thread and the fine woven linen manifested in the gate of the Tabernacle's court show us the works of Jesus Christ in the New Testament's time that have saved the mankind. In this way, the Old Testament's Word of the Tabernacle and the Word of the New Testament are closely and definitely related to each other, like fine woven linen. But, unfortunately, this truth has been hidden for a long time to every truth seeker in Christianity.

Coming to this earth, Jesus Christ was baptized by John and shed His blood on the Cross. Without understanding and believing in the gospel of the water and the Spirit, none of us can ever find out the truth revealed in the Tabernacle. We must now learn this truth of the Tabernacle and believe in it. We all need to realize and believe in the truth manifested in the blue, purple, and scarlet thread and the fine woven linen of the gate of the Tabernacle's court.

The TABERNACLE: A Detailed Portrait of Jesus Christ (II)

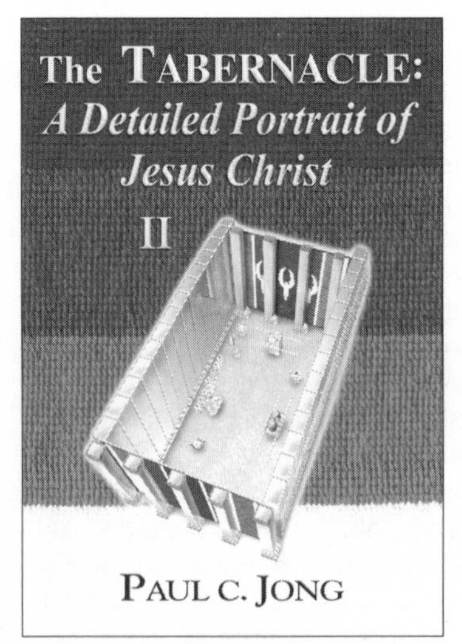

As God had commanded Moses to build the Tabernacle in the Old Testament, in the New Testament, God wants us to also build a Sanctuary in each of our hearts so that He may dwell in us. The material of faith with which we can build this Sanctuary in our hearts is the Word of the gospel of the water and the Spirit. With this gospel of the water and the Spirit, we must wash away all our sins and be cleansed. By telling us to build Him a Sanctuary, God is telling us to empty our hearts and believe in the gospel of the water and the Spirit. We must all cleanse our hearts by believing in the gospel of the water and the Spirit.

When we cleanse away all the sins of our hearts by believing in this gospel Truth, God then comes to dwell in them. It is by believing in this true gospel that you can build the holy Temples in your hearts. It is highly likely that until now, at least some of you have probably been offering your prayers of repentance to cleanse your hearts, trying to build the Temples by yourselves. But now is the time for you to abandon this false faith and be transformed by the renewing of your minds by believing in the gospel of the water and the Spirit.

The Gospel of Matthew (I) & (II)

There are countless new Christians throughout the world, who have just been born again by believing in the gospel of the water and the Spirit that we have been spreading. We are indeed yearning to feed on the bread of life to them. But it is difficult for them to have fellowship with us in the true gospel, for they are all far away from us.

Therefore, to meet the spiritual needs of these people of Jesus Christ, the King of kings, The author proclaims that those who have received the remission of their sins by believing in the Word of Jesus Christ, must feed on His pure Word in order to defend their faith and sustain their spiritual lives. The sermons in these books have been prepared as new bread of life that will nourish the born-again to edify their spiritual growth.

Through His Church and servants, God will continue to provide you with this bread of life. May God's blessings be on all those who have been born again of water and the Spirit, who desires to have true spiritual fellowship with us in Jesus Christ.

The First Epistle of John (I) & (II)

He who believes that Jesus, who is God and the Savior, came by the gospel of the water and the Spirit to deliver all sinners from their sins, is saved from all his sins, and becomes a child of God the Father.

The First Epistle of John states that Jesus, who is God, came to us by the gospel of the water and the Spirit, and that He is the Son of God the Father. The Book, in other words, mostly emphasizes that Jesus is God (1 John 5:20), and concretely testifies the gospel of the water and the Spirit in chapter 5.

We must not hesitate to believe that Jesus Christ is God and to follow Him.

Sermons on Galatians: From Physical Circumcision to the Doctrine of Repentance (I)

Today's Christianity has turned into merely a world religion. Most Christians nowadays live in a situation of being sinners because they haven't been born again by spiritual faith. It is because they have only relied on Christian doctrines without being aware of the gospel of the water and the Spirit until now.

Therefore, now is the time for you to know the spiritual fallacies of the circumcisionists and keep distance from such faith. You have to know the contradictoriness of the prayers of repentance. Now is the time for you to stand firmer than ever on the gospel of the water and the Spirit.

If you haven't believed in this true gospel so far, you have to believe in our Savior who came to us by the gospel of the water and the Spirit even now. Now, you have to be complete Christians with the faith of believing in the gospel Truth of the water and the Spirit.

Memo

Memo

Memo